W9-BKK-858

THREE FACES
OF HERMENEUTICS

Roy J. Howard

Three Faces of Hermeneutics

An Introduction to Current Theories
of Understanding

University of California Press

Berkeley   Los Angeles   London

University of California Press
Berkeley and Los Angeles, California
University of California Press, Ltd.
London, England
Copyright© 1982 by The Regents of the
University of California
Printed in the United States of America
1 2 3 4 5 6 7 8 9

Library of Congress Cataloging in Publication Data

Howard, Roy J.
    Three faces of hermeneutics.

    Bibliography: p. 177
    Includes index.
    1. Hermeneutics. I. Title.
BD241.H73   121'.68   78-66007
ISBN 0-520-03851-7   AACR2

for Stacy, Karin, and Stephen

Contents

Preface

Two reasons suggest the usefulness of a book on philosophical hermeneutics. One is the opportunity to satisfy in part a natural curiosity about some major trends
in European philosophy. The other, more speculative,
is the need to ask about the present status of the continuing debate between the sciences and the humanities.
The heart of this debate has always been the question,
To what degree do the purposes and intentions of the
individual affect the experiences he has, and consequently the shape of the reality he apprehends, and consequently the knowledge he claims to acquire? On the
one hand, science, its lesson learned from Galileo, answers in general that teleology and purposiveness must
be rejected as elements in an explanation; neutrality and
objectivity require that the role of the individual be
discounted as much as possible. Spokesmen for the humanities, on the other hand, are prone to insist that
there are some fields of study—history, for example, or
literature—where the individual's goals, perceptions,
and imagination are so intrinsically involved in the
shape of the reality apprehended that discounting these
would be equivalent to denying that these fields of
study exist at all and would amount to an arbitrary
impoverishment of the world we hope to render intelligible. The issue is far from resolved. Western thinkers
continue to muddle through in the Cold-War-ish antag-
onisms of what Lord Snow in his 1959 Rede lecture
called "The Two Cultures."

Snow in that lecture did not imagine—did not, in fact, desire—that the "two cultures" should some day coalesce into one. He suggested, rather, that the two would better protect their own integrity and would make a more serious contribution to the welfare of the race if each would take the trouble to become better acquainted with the other. Snow was not free of bias in his educational prescription: he thought that the humanities have rather more to learn from the sciences than the other way around. It is a prejudice commonly met in Anglo–American philosophy. Is it justified? The belief fattens on the impression that the claims of science are relatively straightforward and its successes measurable. The claims of the historian and of the littérateur, in contrast, seem notoriously unstable and controversial. The reason, of course, is that the changeableness—fickleness, if you will—of the individual mind is not included in the object that the scientist studies (hence the relative stability of his results), but it is a part of the object investigated by the student of history or of the arts. Is there, all the same, some legitimacy in the latter's claim that in experiencing such purpose-ridden and imaginative manifestations one can gain a genuine insight into human reality, perhaps of a kind that science, by its neutral methods, is precluded from finding? If so, what must be the nature of the experience in which such a special knowledge surfaces? How does it work after coming to consciousness? How is it connected with the way knowledge is acquired in the sciences, so that the general impulse of human intelligence can be seen, and the world described, as a unified, if varicolored, process?

These are the issues alive today in the debate between

the sciences and the humanities. Expressed in nine-teenth-century terminology, it is a debate between those who promote "explanation-theory" exclusively and those who promote, besides "explanation-theory," some form of "understanding-theory." The former hold that the explanatory procedures of the sciences are a necessary and sufficient model for a philosophy of knowledge. The latter maintain that such explanatory procedures may be necessary but are not sufficient and that another kind of procedure is necessary, which they term "understanding." In Blake's words, "Twofold always. May God us keep / From single vision and Newton's sleep."

It is clear today that those philosophers who wish to promote some sort of theory of understanding are on the defensive. To the degree that they are, the humanities, as a separate but equal realm of knowledge, are also on the defensive. This is a theoretical point. It is also practically clear that this theoretical plight of the humanities has a sharper, more biting dimension in the fact that today's complex societies need more and better planning of the sort that science seems to promise, and have less and less money available for supporting the humanities. If, for one reason or another, fewer good minds take up careers in the humanities—as Lord Snow seemed implicitly to recommend—will it be only a measure of embellishment and charm that will diminish in society, or will some more fundamental source of value be lost? Is there a range of truth that the humanities are uniquely empowered to convey? The extensive and sometimes acrimonious discussion which followed Lord Snow's lecture did not throw much light on this question, though it was the heart of the matter.

At the same time as the "two cultures" debate was going on in English and American journals, a book appeared in Germany which resurrected one of the key conceptions of nineteenth-century "understanding-theory." The book was Professor Gadamer's *Truth and Method*. The concept again brought to the fore was hermeneutics. This was a different notion of hermeneutics from any used previously. It owed something to existentialist philosophy, for existentialism has always insisted that the value system of the individual contributed something to, and was therefore partly responsible for, the shape that reality was thought to have. This view took extreme proportions in Sartre, but it was Martin Heidegger's more calm ontological analysis of individual existence which directly influenced Gadamer's notion. (Gadamer was a student of Heidegger.) A fresh light was given to the Husserlian insight that meanings are structures which a person lives before he thinks about them. The idea that an individual, by the fact of his human existence itself, was already a special decoder of reality, already an active interpreter of a peculiar kind, was analyzed. This is why Gadamer's resurrection of the term 'hermeneutics'—which had always meant the study and practice of the art of interpretation—was appropriate.

Gadamer's book provoked a considerable reaction in Germany and one or two isolated echoes in the United States. The subsequent discussion has taken up again the themes, both theoretical and pragmatic, surfacing in Lord Snow's lecture, only this time at an explicitly philosophical level. This should give the topic considerable appeal to those concerned with a philosophy of humanistic education. What, from the point of view of a contribution to our stock of knowledge, is special about the humanities? Even if the pattern of their work is not scientific in the same way as that of physics or chemistry, does it not have a kind of rigor of its own? Must all science be "exact"—that is, quantified—science? These questions about knowledge and reality are philosophers' questions. Raised in the arena of the humanities, where purpose and imagination play such a large role, they are questions about the possibility of having a theory of understanding which is somehow different from a theory of explanation. This book reviews the thought of some philosophers who think, to one degree or another, that such a theory of understanding is viable. Because they are sucessors of nineteenth-century hermeneutical approaches, they could be called, in a very loose sense, 'hermeneuticists.' (I shall try to make this description more precise in the course of the book.) And because their work deals with the essential nature of man and thus responds to the criteria of universality and depth traditionally associated with a philosophical pursuit, their work is philosophical. This is a book about such a philosophical hermeneutics.

Formerly, 'hermeneutics' referred to theory and practice of interpretation. It was a skill one acquired by learning how to use the instruments of history, philology, manuscriptology, and so on. The skill was typically deployed against texts rendered problematic by the ravages of time, by cultural differences, or by the accidents of history. As such, hermeneutics was a regional and occasional necessity—a subdiscipline in theology, archaeology, literary studies, the history of art, and so forth.

In our own day, however—and in addition to the

above—the term has taken on a new sense. It no longer designates a merely subsidiary pursuit. A quantum jump of sorts has taken place, but one of kind and not merely of degree. In the hands of many, hermeneutics may often now be found exercised at a level of generality that clearly stamps it as a philosophical matter.

There are two broad ways in which our contemporaries pursue philosophical hermeneutics. These are distinguished by their main sources of inspiration.

One approach is rooted in linguistics. It begins with the revolutionary work of Ferdinand de Saussure, is influenced by formal studies of Russian and Czechoslovakian provenance, and has sympathetic echoes in the work of Noam Chomsky. This approach is usually called not "hermeneutics" but "structuralism."

The other is rooted in the more explicitly philosophical traditions of Hegel and Marx, of phenomenology, and of linguistic analysis.

This book does not attempt an account of what could be, though it is not often, called "structuralist hermeneutics." The reason is that structuralism, in a widespread reading of its spokesmen, is inclined to defuse the role of the individual in favor of that of transcendental "grammars"—whether in language proper (e.g., Chomsky), in cultural patterns (e.g., Lévi-Strauss), or in stylistics and literary theory (e.g., Fowler, Barthes, Todorov)—hence the "disappearance of man/author" theme sometimes expressed in structuralist writings. In spite of undeniable overlappings between this and the other stream of philosophical hermeneutics, it seems that a structuralist hermeneutics is essentially rationalistic and Kantian, where the other form, in its conceding decisive importance to the individual consciousness, remains individualistic and Hegelian (see for example Hoy 1978, pp. 132–133, 144–146). The title of this book, therefore, and the subsequent use of "hermeneutics" and its cognates refer to a philosophical theory of understanding developed out of Hegelian/Marxist, phenomenological, or analytical sources.

One final remark. Some, already acquainted with recent literature in the field, may be surprised to find enrolled here under the banner of hermeneutics certain Wittgensteinian or analytic philosophers. It is true, the label is used for practical purposes almost universally for certain trends in Continental philosophy and not for those in Anglo–American philosophy. But Karl-Otto Apel, in a convincing historical thesis, argues that there is a clear and profound "connection between the Analytical problem of 'understanding language' and the problem of 'understanding' as seen by the [Continental] Geisteswissenschaften" (Apel 1967, p. 3). And the Finnish philosopher Georg Henrik von Wright—himself a spokesman in the Wittgensteinian or analytic tradition—suggests that using 'hermeneutical' to include also the late or antipositivist Wittgensteinians serves to sharpen the distinction between the positivist and antipositivist analytical camps and does "more justice to the morphology of trends in contemporary thought" than would the confining of 'hermeneutical' to variations on a purely phenomenological theme (von Wright 1971, p. 182 n. 86). The suggestion is, in other words, that anti-positivist analytical philosophers have more in common with their phenomenological colleagues than with the positivist wings of their own empiricist tradition. If this can be substantiated, one of the scandals of contemporary philosophy, the wall of in-

comprehension between Anglo–American and Continental philosophers, may begin to come down. (It is, in
fact, a distant purpose of this book to aid in such a
dismantling.)

The present work cannot claim to be an exhaustive
treatment, neither in the sense of reporting all current
forms of hermeneutics nor in that of leaving nothing
unsaid of the three traditions considered. It is a selection
and an interpretation, an exploratory mapping of ave-
nues in the tradition presented. The first chapter considers developments within the analytic tradition as it
has been influenced by the work of the early and later
Wittgenstein. This chapter comes first because it makes
most clearly a point common to all the hermeneuticists:
the rejection of a mono-methodological empiricism. It
also clearly presents the case for the inescapability of
"subjective" input while avoiding, for all that, a sub-
sidence into psychologism. Chapter two, rejecting the
mono-methodologism both of positivism and of classi-
cal Marxism, reports the speculation of an evolved and
more adequate Marxism which incorporates some
methodological lessons from the symbol-deciphering
work of Freud. The spokesman here is the Frankfurt
philosopher Jürgen Habermas. Chapter three reports a
phenomenological development as found in the seminal reflections of Professor Gadamer. The book begins
with an Introduction which sketches historically the
origin of philosophical hermeneutics in the nineteenth
century. It was then that the discipline came to a philosophical awareness of itself in striving to make a constructive response to the challenges of Kantian, and
later of positivist epistemologies.

I wish to acknowledge the stimulation and encouragement given this book by students, by colleagues, and by Bob Zachary and Jack Miles, editors at the University of California Press. Particular thanks are due to Jørgen Haas and Karen Skov, colleagues at Odense University (Denmark), where I had the pleasure of a semester's exchange professorship. They and Tom Weston of my home university contributed many useful criticisms and suggestions. I am also grateful to our secretaries, Cindy Haupt and Barbara MacCormac, for taking on the burden of typing and proofreading the manuscript. Needless to say, the deficiencies that remain must be attributed to myself. Finally, I wish to make the following copyright acknowledgments: Cornell University Press for permission to quote from Georg H. von Wright's *Explanation and Understanding,* copyright © 1971 by Cornell University Press; Columbia University Press for permission to quote from G. H. von Wright's *Causality and Determinism,* copyright © 1974 by Columbia University Press; Routledge and Kegan Paul Ltd. and their USA representative Humanities Press Inc. for permission to quote from Peter Winch's *The Idea of Social Science and Its Relation to Philosophy,* copyright © 1958 by Routledge and Kegan Paul Ltd.; Beacon Press for permission to quote from Jürgen Habermas's *Knowledge and Human Interests,* copyright © 1971 by Beacon Press; Sheed and Ward Ltd. for permission to quote from Hans Georg Gadamer's *Truth and Method,* English translation copyright © 1975 by Sheed and Ward Ltd., used with permission of the Continuum Publishing Company.

Roy J. Howard ☐

Philosophy Department
San Diego State University

The kind of philosophy one chooses depends upon what sort of person he is. A philosophical system is not a lifeless collection of odds and ends that could be discarded or retained at whim. It is animated, rather, by the soul of the man who holds it.

Fichte □

Introduction:
Origins of the Problem

Hermeneutics will not appear as a typical listing in a catalog of university studies. The field is usually thought of as a subdiscipline for theology, where it covers the study of methods for the authentication and interpretation of texts. This is the sense of the word's earliest appearance in English, as demonstrated by the 1737 entry in the *Oxford English Dictionary,* "Taking such liberties with sacred writ, as are by no means allowable upon any known rules of just and sober hermeneuticks." There has always been a theology associated with hermeneutics because of the interest that dogma has in the interpretation of scripture. But, except in the indirect way in which theology may influence or be influenced by philosophy, there was not in earlier centuries a distinctly philosophical kind of hermeneutics.

This step was taken in the nineteenth century, particularly with the work of Friedrich Schleiermacher and Wilhelm Dilthey. They used the term "hermeneutics" in conjunction with their effort to find a theory of knowledge for the data with which the cultural scientist works—such things as texts, signs and symbols of various sorts, rituals, images, examples of the fine and the useful arts—in short, for such products as are the result rather of man's deliberate ingenuity than of nature's blind working. Schleiermacher and Dilthey had no quarrel with the philosophy then developed for the natural sciences. In token of this they accepted a separate nomenclature for their work. They called theirs the effort to find a theory for "understanding," an intellectual activity seen as differing both in object and in form from "explaining." Their work in the long run was more successful in highlighting the problem than in finding a solution. After their deaths few carried on the quest. Recently there has been a resurgence of interest in the question they raised, sparked especially by the appearance in 1960 of Hans-Georg Gadamer's *Wahrheit und Methode* (see Gadamer 1975*a*), a work which has occasioned much fruitful discussion (see Bubner 1970). More recently the discussion has expanded to become an epistemological pursuit of the purest sort, as for example at the 1974 conference in Helsinki on the topic of "Explanation and Understanding" (see Manninen 1976).

Why, one might ask, adopt the somewhat pedantic term "hermeneutics" for this new focus in philosophy? Why not simply stay with the more traditional term "epistemology"?

There is not, I submit, any totally convincing reason for accepting the new label. One can adduce the desire of certain spokesmen to signify their allegiance in one degree or another to the perspective developed by Dilthey and so to distinguish themselves from the unidimensional and reductivist approaches of certain forms of empiricist epistemology. One can also point out that speech—whose interpretation was always hermeneutics' precise goal—lies clearly at the center of current philosophical reflection. Indeed, grammatical categories are thought by many to be operative in one's first experience, and hence decoding, of the world. "Hermeneutics," then, traditionally described as the art of interpreting language, is not a bad name for this focus in current epistemology. In particular, it does have the virtue of connoting a nonpositivist philosophy of man. This philosophy views him as having something special in his noetic behavior, a quality that is not simply on a continuum with nonhuman nature and which is, in fact, the source of that realm of value or freedom or responsibility, whose visible signs are man's social institutions and culture.

My purpose in this introduction is to trace briefly the migration of hermeneutics from its subsidiary role in theology to its present status as a general name for current studies favoring the hypothesis of something special in the epistemology of "understanding." This migration is propelled noticeably by three forces: the influence of Kant, the role of Dilthey, and the challenge of logical positivisim.

The Influence of Kant

Kant's hand is decisive for contemporary hermeneutics, explicitly so among the continental hermeneuticists and in an "unseen" fashion among those of an analytic or formal turn of mind. It is as though Kant, in his argument with Hume, fired the most telling barrage in a confrontation that still pits hermeneuticists against a certain form of empiricism.

Kant's question may be formulated this way: Granted that reliable knowledge occurs, what are the conditions necessary for its occurrence? Two features of his answer are decisive for contemporary hermeneutics. The first is the role he assigns to the natural sciences in epistemology. The second is his analysis of the way in which the subject and object function in the exercise of knowing. The first point may be quickly summarized, for Kant is far from being the first philosopher to adopt this tack.

Kant assigns to the experience of knowing in the natural sciences a normative role for the rest of epistemology. In the preface to the second edition of the *Critique of Pure Reason* he recalls Galileo, Torricelli, and Stahl, and says that these "students of nature"

learned that reason has insight only into that which it produces after a plan of its own, and that it must not allow itself to be kept, as it were, in nature's leading strings, but must itself show the way with principles of judgment based upon fixed laws, constraining nature to give answer to questions of reason's own determining. . . . [Reason must play the role] of an appointed judge who compels the witnesses to answer questions which he has himself formulated. . . . It is thus that the study of nature has entered on the secure path of a science, after having for so many centuries been nothing but a process of merely random groping. [Kant 1968, pp. 20–21]

The metaphor of judge, court, and witnesses compelled to testify is deeply symptomatic of Kant's epistemology. The logic of inquiry manifested in the procedures of the natural sciences will turn out to be the statute book for the necessary conditions of knowing generally. Metaphysics, for example, will no longer have a standing as a theoretically viable realm of truth; it will have to be content with an acceptance stemming from practical considerations. Kant's second Copernican revolution, then, refashions a traditional aim in philosophy—the search for a unified and homogeneous ideal of knowing—but it does so at the risk of making such knowing as was supposed to occur in the non-scientific realms theoretically untenable and only emotionally, psychologistically—in short, irrationally—tolerable. How this comes about is shown in the second feature of Kant's thought, which is critical for current discussions in hermeneutics: the roles played by the subject and the object in knowing.

"Subject" in this context means the knower—the self, ego, or consciousness—which acquires knowledge of reality. "Object" here means the reality that is known—a non-self in some degree or other—which impinges on the subject and supplies the material that knowledge is about. Their relationship is a process of moving from the haphazard collection of sensations to that ordered synthesis which we call "knowing something." In this synthesis both subject and object play a clearly defined role.

The subject—as Kant's metaphor of the judge suggests—is possessed of "rules which I must presuppose as being in me prior to objects being given to me, and therefore as being *a priori*" (Kant 1968, p. 23). These a priori rules perform a synthesizing function on sensations; they give them a spatial and temporal configuration, for example, and connect them in relations of identity, causality, and so on. Far from being derived from experience, as Hume thought, these pre-given rules are the necessary conditions for having any experience at all—that is, for being able to order sensation into even that initial systematic structure which 'experience' implies. As omnipresent these rules are transcendental: they apply, not to diverse regions of thinking, but to thinking as such. They are the a priori necessary conditions of "pure" reason. The constructivist role which Kant assigns to the subject, then, is what marks his second Copernican revolution in epistemology, his "new method of thought, namely that we can know a priori of things only what we ourselves put into them" (ibid.). Just as Copernicus hypothesized the sun as the determinant of orbits for the rest of the physical universe, Kant located in transcendental consciousness the rules that determined all other forms of knowing.

While Kant's transcendental synthesizing principles supply the form, they do not, however, supply the matter of knowledge. If I say, "Last week's frost caused the tree's leaves to curl and turn black," the spatial and temporal form of this judgment as well as its pattern in terms of substance, accident, causality, and so on, are supplied by the mind; but the factual content of this judgment—what makes it a candidate for being true of the world—is supplied uniquely by sensation. To that degree Hume is correct. Whether there was indeed a frost last week and whether this was the factor causing the leaves to turn black are matters for empirical verification, not for a priori reasoning. The particularity of my judgment is not only not logically necessary, it cannot be. The synthesizing forces of the mind are merely forms, interpretative grids impressing themselves upon the appearances of objects. What indigenous structure objects may have in themselves we cannot know: "Things in themselves would necessarily, apart from any understanding that knows them, conform to laws of their own. But appearances are only representations of things which are unknown with regard to what they may be in themselves. As mere representations they are subject to no law of connection save that which the connecting faculty prescribes" (Kant 1968, p. 172).

This applies to the self, when considered as an object in nature, as well as to objects other than the self. Kant, consequently, needs two senses of "self": one, an empirical self who has a name and social security number, a nationality, a sex, and a culture—a history, in short—and another, a transcendental self, a "self-form" or regulatory system, who makes possible the synthesizing of our discrete experiences into a personal history: "There can be in us no modes of knowledge, no connection or unity of one mode of knowledge with another, without that unity of consciousness which precedes all data of intuitions, and by relation to which representation of objects is alone possible. This pure original unchangeable consciousness I shall name *transcendental apperception*" (Kant 1968, p. 136).

Kant's transcendental subject, then, is seen as a pure, logical, ahistorical regulatory system. The empirical subject is its appearance in space and time, a synthesis effected by transcendental consciousness of "inner" states. Correlative with this ego–synthesis of inner states is the object. The object, the "thing" that we know, is a synthesis, effected by consciousness, of "outer" states received in sensation. Subject and object obviously involve each other and always function together. But just as clearly, they are not the same thing. The transcendental ego stands as a preinstructed organizer against the wash of appearances. Thanks to its organizing function, appearances are turned into objects of knowledge.

More recent work in hermeneutics is characterized by its reaction to these two features of Kantian epistemology: its unitary version of knowing, which implies that apparently different logics of inquiry must in reality have the same essential pattern; and its description of the ahistorical role assigned the subject, which implies that the knower is either endowed with or can methodologically postulate a point of view "outside" the world in order to reason about it. Two complex catalysts trigger this reaction, leading to nineteenth-century and twentieth-century versions of hermeneutics. The nineteenth-century catalysts were the anti-Kantian critiques of Comte and Mill, from the side of empiricism, and of Hegel, from the side of metaphysics. In the twentieth century the catalysts are logical positivism, from the side of the logic of science, and Husserl's phenomenology, from the side of metaphysics. Let us take the nineteenth-century development first. The influences of Comte, Mill, and Hegel show up well in the work of Wilhelm Dilthey—"the father of hermeneutics," as he is often called.

The Role of Dilthey

For his part, Dilthey would prefer assigning this title to the philologist–theologian–philosopher Friedrich Schleiermacher (1768–1834), "a mind," he writes, "where a virtuoso practice of philological interpretation was united with a genuine capacity for philosophical thought" (Dilthey 1972, p. 240). A word about Schleiermacher's contribution will make Dilthey's position clearer.

In his work on Greek and biblical texts, Schleiermacher had come to realize that the tools of the philologist succeeded in illuminating only the surface or "vocabulary" levels of the text—the "grammatical" or "comparative" levels, as he called them. Of themselves they failed to reveal the author's special insight, which was the reason for the composition in the first place, and was what gave the parts of the composition their unity. This deeper, spiritual level of the work Schleiermacher called the "divinatory" or "psychological" level.

Understanding an author, then, Schleiermacher argues, means more than understanding his words. It means understanding the spirit which initiated and controlled his writing, and for whose representation the writing exists. After all, the author's vocabulary was a possession shared with his contemporaries. So was that wider "vocabulary," the scientific and cultural environment in which he lived. What is noteworthy about the author's work—and the basis of its survival—is what he does with this common possession, the insight he has into it and the fresh way he organizes it. It took a kind of "divination" for the author to achieve this. It takes a corresponding kind of divination for the interpreter to appreciate it.

This implies, as Schleiermacher saw, that the unifying insight of the author, a totality, must somehow be present in each portion of the work's composition. It is an inner dynamic, like that in a bead of mercury which, even when its original mass is shattered, continues in its fractions to manifest the same shape. Of course, the interpreter can only begin with a part, but even there it is the whole he is looking for, the whole with which the author started and which now lies concealed in the parts. The actual practice of hermeneutics becomes a part–whole–part movement, a constant back and forth or dialectical process. This movement, which begins where it will end, is, in geometry, a circular movement. It describes the famous "hermeneutic circle" (see Hoy 1978, p. 2 ff.).

This experience of understanding supposes a process whereby the total meaning of one insightful individual is linearized in common expressions and then recapturable by a different, perhaps very different, individual.

The problem is both practical and theoretical. Practically, what is the content of the author's message to us? Theoretically, what are the conditions that make it possible for the author's message—or any message—to reach us? As philologist, Schleiermacher exercised with brilliance his practical skills on the texts of Plato and of St. Paul. As philosopher, however, he realized that, for interpretation to be sound, one must bring clearly to light the conceptual factors involved in such exercises of interpretation. Only then could one have some confidence that caprice is avoided and a measure of objectivity attained. In formulating and attempting to resolve this latter question, Schleiermacher shifted the problem of hermeneutics to its present general and philosophical level.

It is usually said that he essayed an answer to this question in a psychologistic and therefore ultimately unsatisfactory fashion. This judgment on his work need not concern us here. It suffices to note that, after Schleiermacher, hermeneutics became an epistemological and theoretical and no longer a merely methodological and practical endeavor.

As one can see from Dilthey's remark cited earlier, Schleiermacher impressed his contemporaries with the unity of his practice and thought. It was clearly this integration of mind and life which inspired his biographer and intellectual successor, Wilhelm Dilthey (1833-1911). A Romantic in spirit himself, Dilthey was bound to sympathize with Schleiermacher's "divinatory" ideal. At the same time there was a more pronounced note of empiricism in Dilthey's thought. He judged Schleiermacher's categories to be too Platonic, too inadequately based in history, to offer a firm footing for objective interpretation in the human sciences (cf. Ermarth 1975, p. 244). He set out to find a better basis. Two great influences, Kant and empiricism, shaped his early thought. Along with the majority of his thoughtful colleagues in Germany, Dilthey acknowledged the superiority of Kant's analyses, which combined a general approach to espistemology in terms of necessary principles with an admission, consistent with empiricist approaches, that actual knowledge can only come from experience. This linking of the necessary and the contingent was the key point. Of course, anti-Kantian forces were in motion as well.

Dilthey's own researches, in fact, were beginning just as positivism as an identifiable school in philosophy was breaking upon the intellectual scene. Auguste Comte, in his *Cours de philosophie positive* (1830), had argued that, just as laws had been found for the interaction of elements in nature, so, and by the same methods, they could be found for the interactions of men in society. The physics of mechanical movements uncovered in nonhuman systems would be complemented by a "social physics" for humans. With this in place, the unified "philosophical system of the moderns will be in fact complete" (Comte 1896, I:6).

An even more telling thesis for a single methodology of knowledge came from the English philosopher John Stuart Mill, whose *System of Logic* was published in 1843. It was translated into German in 1863, with the pregnant feature that Mill's phrase "Moral Sciences" in the heading of Book VI was rendered into German by the newly coined term, *Geisteswissenschaften*—"human sciences," as we have elected to translate it back into English.

Explicitly in opposition to Kant's thesis of a priori synthesizing principles, Mill argues that these are instead derived solely from the association of repeated experiences. That these laws take shape at the psychic level does not imply that they are a priori to consciousness or self-generated. There are laws of thinking, of the formation of principles, in the same way as there are laws of external nature. And this holds true for a society's set of customs and attitudes as much as it does for an individual's set of logical or arithmetical judgments: "All phenomena of society are phenomena of human nature, generated by the action of outward circumstances upon masses of human beings; and if, therefore, the phenomena of human thought, feeling, and action are subject to fixed laws, the phenomena of society cannot but conform to fixed laws, the consequence of the preceding" (Mill 1884, p. 607).

Dilthey was distinctly interested in the newly emerging field of psychology, on which Comte and Mill were placing such stress. At the home of a friend he took part in a set of informal seminars largely concerned with the views of these empiricist philosophers. The discussions were sympathetic to the ideal of objectivity for the human sciences espoused by positivism as well as to its thesis, that all truth derives from experience. At the same time, Dilthey was too aware of Kant's critique of Hume to be able to conclude, with Mill, that the laws of thought could be reduced to the passive registering of sensations and the later conversion of these in some way into necessary principles. It was not the empiricism of Comte and Mill that Dilthey rejected so much as the inadequacy of their view—particularly Mill's—that associationist psychology of the type then current could supply a foundation for objectivity in the human sciences. Dilthey, in fact, saw his question in essentially the same terms as Kant had conceived his, only applied now to the field of the human sciences: How does reliable knowledge in this area occur? He could not simply tranpose Kant's ahistorical 'self' to the field of history. It shared, but from the opposite side, a fault with the empiricists: "No real blood flows in the veins of the knowing subject constructed by Locke, Hume, and Kant; it is only the diluted juice of reason, a mere process of thought" (Dilthey 1976, p. 162). Dilthey made it his lifelong ambition to complement Kant's *Critiques* of pure and practical reason with a "critique of historical reason." Despite many years' effort he never satisfied himself that he had an adequate solution to his problem. The work which was to crown and unify his philosophical career remained unwritten.

The exploratory and unfinished character of Dilthey's extensive writings foreshadows the difficulties interpreters experience in trying to comprehend his thought. Its main lines, however, are clear. There are three points to note here. The first is his distinction between the fields of the natural and human sciences; the second is his thesis of "experience" and "life" as the unifying elements within the field of the human sciences; and the third is his logic for the interpretation of "life" as objectified in historical documents.

As early as 1843, the German historiographer J. G. Droysen, in his efforts to establish the study of history on firmer grounds than those offered by the idealism of Hegel, argued for a sharp distinction between the methods of the natural and historical sciences. *Erklären* ("to explain") was isolated as the epistemological goal of the former; *verstehen* ("to understand") was that of the latter.

Dilthey adopted this distinction, accepting the epistemological problem as partitioned in the way Droysen had done it. The foundations of knowledge for the natural sciences were not his concern. He accepted the Kantian analysis when applied to that area:

These laws can only be found when the vivid character of our impressions of nature, the continuity we sense with it, in as much as we are ourselves natural, and the lively feeling with which we enjoy it increasingly retreat behind an abstract conception of it according to relations of space, time, mass, and motion. All these moments work together for the shunting aside of man himself, in order to construct from his impression of the great object, nature, an arrangement according to laws. [Dilthey 1914–, VII: 82–83]

It was precisely because nature *could* be viewed as this "non-self" and impersonal object, as an order "shunting man aside," that it was possible to interpret nature in the explanatory terms of mathematical and ahistorical principles. But, in contrast, what is characteristic of our experience of cultural phenomena is precisely our sense that these cannot be relegated to a "non-self" category, that they exist, rather, as "for-us" kinds of phenomena, and that the attempt to relegate them to the category of non-human systems—which can of course logically be made and which Mill was in fact making—empties them of the character that makes them special. In short, Dilthey maintained that an objective handling of cultural phenomena must respect their relational, "for-us" character and hence must accept the cultural object as existing in a special system which contains as part the historical self for whom the object exists. To this intuited quality of the cultural object as constituted by a continuity with one's own psychic structures Dilthey gave the name *Zusammenhang,* "connectedness."

The human sciences are distinguished from the natural sciences in that the latter take as their object features which appear to consciousness as coming from outside, as phenomena, and as given in particulars; for the former, in contrast, the object appears as coming from within, as a reality, and as a vivid original whole. It follows therefore that for the natural sciences an ordering of nature is achieved only through a succession of conclusions by means of linking of hypotheses. For the human sciences, on the contrary, it follows that the connectedness of psychic life is given as an original and general foundation. Nature we explain, the life of the soul we understand. [Dilthey 1914–, V: 143–144]

How can we explain the connectedness or "for-us" structuring that takes place in the apprehension of the human phenomena? Dilthey adopted a word already familiar in the writings of the Romantics and gave it a firmer philosophical status: *Erlebnis,* often translated as "lived experience." What marks an experience as "lived" (rather than, say, as merely endured) is its immediate fitting into the patterns of significance which we already entertain about our own lives or about that extension of them which is society. Such experiences have in them an immediately apprehended note of purpose, intention, meaning—significance in the strong psychic sense of the term:

The connectedness of experience in its concrete reality lies in the category of significance. This is the unity that brings together into memory the course of what has been experienced or re-experienced. And the significance of this does not consist in a point of unity lying outside experience. Rather, this significance is constitutively contained in these experiences as their connectedness. [Dilthey 1914–, VII: 237]

The difference from Kant at this point is notable. It is not an ahistorical regulatory system that synthesizes cultural impressions into an experience: this category of understanding springs from the ebb and flow of life itself. It involves particular memories of items and events in one's own history. There is no transcendental point from which to view the human phenomena:

> Our understanding of life is only a constant approxima-tion; that life reveals quite different sides to us according to the point of view from which we consider its course in time is due to the nature of both understanding and life. [Dilthey 1961, p. 109]

It is often said that Dilthey, especially in his early writings, "psychologizes" (i.e., reduces to affective terms) the interpreting process in the human sciences and hence makes empathy an essential ingredient of understanding-theory. Recent scholarship suggests that this view is mistaken (cf. Makkreel 1975, p. 252 n. 5; Ermarth 1976, pp. 170 ff., 232 ff.). Of his position in his later writings, at any rate, there should be no doubt. The experience Dilthey speaks of there, even though it is described as "an inner reality, a coherence experienced from within," is considered to be of a "fixed" object, "one that we can return to again and again" and try to understand in "an orderly and sys-tematic" manner—one, in short, whose study is deter-mined by "common conditions and epistemological instruments, [and which] must everywhere present the same characteristics" (Dilthey 1972, pp. 231–232). No doubt Dilthey's sense of *Erlebnis,* as a purposeful and value-filled moment of life, has its affective side; but that its import for him was mainly noetic and epistemological there can be no doubt.

This introduces the third feature of Dilthey's thought which we here consider—the objectivation of meaning in symbols.

This is a Hegelian note in Dilthey, especially prominent in his later years—an empiricist version, one might call it, of Hegel's *"objektiver Geist."* If the previous section could be seen as the epistemological or subjective moment of Dilthey's position, this section may be seen as its objective or ontological component. It will be helpful to introduce this section by reviewing some aspects of Hegel's critique of Kant.

Hegel had attacked Kant in precisely those two features that we mentioned earlier. He argued that an unprejudiced critique of knowing cannot begin by assuming one area of experience as normative. It may be true that the philosopher is psychologically attracted by the example of the "secure path of science" and repelled by the "groping" character of much else that passes for knowledge. But Kant revealed prejudice in his preference for science: he already possessed specific notions about what knowledge was and about the roles played in it by subject and object. His call for a renewed critique of metaphysics based on the models of mathematics and science is a symptom of this. It is true that a critique of knowledge must begin somewhere, but Hegel's contention is that it must begin not with a settled thesis of what counts as knowledge but rather with the opposite view that one does not know what knowledge is and so remains open to noticing the forms that knowing itself adopts. If one practices this method of openness to experience—or phenomenology—it is possible for consciousness to catch sight of its own coming to knowledge:

. . . we shall here undertake the exposition of knowledge as a phenomenon. . . . Phenomenal knowledge can be regarded as the path of the soul, which is traversing the series of its own forms of embodiment, like stages appointed for it by its own nature, that it may possess the clearness of spiritual life when, through the complete experience of its own self, it arrives at the knowledge of what it is in itself. [Hegel 1931, p. 135]

Within this series of dynamic shapes and not outside it, both self and object emerge as foci, revealing an "in-it-self" and a "for-us" variety of being:

[What] at first appeared as object is reduced, when it passes into consciousness, to what knowledge takes it to be, and the implicit nature, the real in itself, becomes what this entity *per se* is *for consciousness;* this latter is the new object, whereupon there appears also a new mode or embodiment of consciousness, of which the essence is something other than that of the preceding mode. It is this circumstance which carries forward the whole succession of the modes or attitudes of consciousness in their own necessity. It is only this necessity, this origination of the new object—which offers itself to consciousness without consciousness knowing how it comes by it—that to us, who watch the process, is to be seen going on, so to say, behind its back. . . . [For] *it,* what has thus arisen has merely the character of object, while, *for us,* it appears at the same time as a process and coming into being. [Hegel 1931, p. 144]

This is what a Hegelian phenomenology of mind reveals.

Where Kant's metaphor for the knower was that of the preinstructed judge, then, Hegel's is that of the plant—only, a conscious one—evolving from stage to stage towards self-fulfillment. But Hegel had his prejudice, too, which was the assumption of an absolute mind at once guiding and emerging in this process. This absolute mind played "behind man's back," one may say, the Kantian role of a transcendental consciousness. Becoming is the approximation of this mind; being is its emergence. Being and mind are ultimately one.

Dilthey does not accept this idealistic identification of mind and being. The exploratory nature of understanding mentioned earlier, which he learned from practicing historians like Droysen, Schleiermacher, and Ranke, protected him from thinking that "objectivated mind" or our own apprehension of history is in the service of an absolute and fundamentally ahistorical spirit. The groping nature of knowledge and of its expressions is an intrinsic and not a cancellable feature of its being. It is not absolute meaning, therefore, that Dilthey expects to find surfacing in the cultural legacy of history, but only a finite and limited meaning appropriate to the time. This indicates the empiricist nature of Dilthey's hermeneutics. The "mind" expressed in those data which are the products of man's intentions is not an absolute mind secreted in time, but the finite mind of this actual person or that, of this actual society or that.

In his own methodology, Dilthey echoes the logic of Schleiermacher's hermeneutic circle in a wider sphere. It is still the part–whole–part movement, but now the individual's life can be seen as condensing somehow the whole of society, in the same way as one experience within an individual's life can assume the status of a totalizing moment for his whole life: "the connectedness of a life can only be understood through the meaning the individual parts have for understanding the whole and . . . every part of the life of mankind can only be understood in the same way" (Dilthey 1961, p. 105).

Interpretation of totality, therefore, must begin with the study of a part. But what "parts" reveal, or make objective, the life of the mind? Human expressions, as we have said, which are externalizations of mind. But which expressions preeminently? Linguistic expressions. It is most notably in them that the totality of cultural meanings may be supposed to reside. Like culture, they have form and yet movement. They are communal and yet individual. Their successful objectification—as opposed to that of the objects of the natural sciences—supposes the intervention of other subjectivities:

The commonality of life unities is the point of departure for all relations of the particular and the general in the human sciences. The fundamental experience of community permeates the entire way of apprehending the cultural world. In this basic experience are combined consciousness of a unitary self and that of a similarity with others, the sameness of human nature together with individuality. This it is, which is the presupposition of understanding. Starting with elementary interpretation, which requires only acquaintance with the meaning of words and the way in which they are combined into sentences according to rules in order to create a meaning—in other words, beginning with a commonality of language and thought—the scope of what is common, which makes possible the development of understanding, continually expands. [Dilthey 1914, VII: 141]

We may summarize Dilthey's contribution to our subject with the following remarks. He accepted Schleiermacher's insight that the problem of hermeneutics was fundamentally an epistemological one and hence belonged to philosophy rather than to philology. He also accepted Droysen's demarcation of the field of knowledge into the areas of the natural sciences, where explanation-theory was the meta-philosophical task, and of the cultural sciences, where understanding-theory was needed. Dilthey thought Kant had accomplished the former. He set himself the task of composing the latter. History, as the most conspicuous record of life and mind, was the primary discipline of the cultural sciences and the proper place to begin. Writings, as the primary objective datum for the historian, became the focus of reflection. Philosophical hermeneutics, then, would be a metatheory of the understanding of life-experiences as they are given in linguistic expression.

This is its status today. At the same time, contemporary philosophical hermeneutics has a problematic almost totally different from the one envisaged by the "father of hermeneutics." The reason lies in the different perspective from which language is studied. Dilthey, in his concentration on the "understanding" function of language and in his assumption that Kant had dissected with fair accuracy the epistemology of the natural sciences, neglected, understandably enough, taking into account new developments in the philosophical theory of language—developments of such consequence that the phrase "revolution in philosophy" was later used to characterize them (cf. Ryle et al. 1957). These developments have enormous impact upon contemporary hermeneutics. A mention of them closes this introduction. For our purposes, the theory of language advocated by the school of logical positivism was the most significant development.

The Challenge
of Logical Positivism

Logical positivism began as a logic for the physical sciences. In 1895 a chair for the philosophy of the inductive sciences was founded at the University of Vienna and first held by Ernst Mach. The position devolved in 1922 to Moritz Schlick, formerly a student of Max Planck but at that time concentrating his work on the philosophy of physics. A like-minded group formed around him, researchers not only from philosophy but also from mathematics and physics. In 1929 this group published a manifesto of its goals and gave itself a name: "A Scientific Conception of the World: the Vienna Circle." Its members were never as homogeneous in their opinions as is sometimes thought; nevertheless, there was unanimity upon certain basic theses.

One of these was the Kant-like assumption that physics was normative for epistemology, in the sense that the *kind* of thing physicists were doing—their use of a "thing-language," to use Carnap's phrase—offered the most conspicuously successful use of language as an instrument for knowing reality. It was hoped that a study of this language would reveal the abstract form of that language by which the nature of reality could be rationally explored. Epistemology be-

came the task of unraveling the mysteries of this ideal
language. Epistemology became, in short, a metatheory of the language of physics:

> To inquire into the logical structure of scientific knowl-
> edge is to inquire into the logical connections of the con-
> cepts and propositions of science. . . . It is this kind of in-
> quiry, the logical analysis of concepts, propositions, proofs,
> hypotheses, theories of science, which constitutes episte-
> mology, indeed, philosophy in general. [Kraft 1953, p. 26]

The monoscientific ideal of Comte and Mill was retained:

> One cannot acquiesce in a juxtaposition in the conceptual
> systems of physics, biology, psychology, sociology, and the
> historical sciences, as though in each of these sciences a
> unique language were spoken. . . . [The] laws and concepts
> of the special sciences must belong to *one* single system,
> they cannot be simply juxtaposed without connection.
> They must constitute a unified science with one conceptual
> system (a language common to all the sciences) containing
> the conceptual systems of the individual sciences as mem-
> bers and their languages as sublanguages. [Kraft 1953, pp.
> 160–161]

Finally, the function played by this ideal language is
analogous to that played by Kant's subject of transcendental apperception. This abstract language could be
called an a priori, for, like logic, it is not derived from
experience, though it contains within itself whatever
valid structures experience can bear witness to: "Language constitutes, so to speak, the body of knowledge;

the latter could not be built up without it" (Kraft 1953, p. 27). The philosophical study of reality thereafter entailed first of all a study of language. With this conclusion, the legacy of Dilthey and that of the new logical positivism were headed on a course of either collision or collaboration.

The Vienna Circle ceased to function as a cohesive school in the late thirties, a consequence more of internal criticisms than of attacks by "outside" sources. The fallout, however, from its initial explosion onto the philosophical scene is still considerable. The scope and methodology of its analytic approach to language has been broadened to include much more than the "thing-language" of physics. Even in the analysis of ordinary language, however, the meticulous, methodical ethos of the Vienna Circle remains. So does its positivistic ideal, if by positivism one means, as von Wright describes it, "a philosophy advocating methodological monism, mathematical ideals of perfec tion, and a subsumption-theoretic [i.e., laws-based] view of scientific explanation" (von Wright 1971, p. 9).

We can date the moment when logical positivism made explicit contact with the hermeneutic question raised by Dilthey. It was in Carl Hempel's 1942 article, "The Function of General Laws in History," a classic position paper, often reprinted, which has ever after served as a reference point for modern debate between the "explanation" and "understanding" schools of philosophy (cf. Hempel 1949).

It is worth pausing here to note the differences with which this moment is viewed by hermeneuticists of the English-oriented and German-oriented traditions.

Von Wright, a spokesman for the former, writes, "In retrospect, it seems almost an irony of fate that the fullest and most lucid formulation of the positivist theory of explanation should have been stated in connection with the subject matter for which, obviously, the theory is least suited, namely history" (von Wright 1971, pp. 10–11). Karl-Otto Apel, on the other hand, does not find it surprising, because in the historical sciences "the method of objectifying actions as events to be causally explained—thus approaching the methods of the natural sciences—can still rather easily take root" (Apel 1967, pp. 20–21). Historical actions, in Apel's view, have a typical means-to-ends pattern which is like the instrumentalist patterns of the natural sciences. A non-instrumentalist "understanding," on the other hand—literature, for example—would constitute a more challenging object for positivist analysis. In any event, it is to historical argumentation and not to literary expression that Hempel turned his attentions.

Hempel's theory continues to show the optimism of Comte and Mill, that laws can in principle be discovered for the behavior of individuals and of societies, but he injects the sophistication that contemporary theories of the language of science afford. His theory—usually called the "covering law model" of historical explanation—holds that an historical event is explained when a set of circumstances antecedent to it can be subsumed under a general law, established from other studies, so that a deductive combination of statements of the law and statements of the circumstances would trigger a statement predicting the event, if not absolutely then with a high degree of probability. For example, the eventual defeat of the South in the Civil War can be explained (could have been predicted) when particular measurements of the superior industrial potential, manpower resources, naval power, and so on of the North (statement of circumstances) are subsumed under a lawlike statement to the effect that "In an armed conflict superiority in human and material resources guarantees victory." If questions arise about the mental attitudes of the belligerents, these too can be answered by explanations of a causal sort, perhaps by economic, psychic, or other conditioning factors. Hempel concedes that little of history is actually written with this degree of exactitude and that, therefore, most historical writing should be called "explanation sketches" rather than explanation properly so called (Hempel 1949, p. 465). This is because the necessary covering laws, chiefly in the area of psychology, have not been established. The historian's lack of interest, in any case, in consulting or encouraging the search for such laws is thought to derive in large part from his mistaken assumption that our access to historical data can satisfactorily occur by way of "the method of empathic understanding" (Hempel 1949, p. 467) rather than by way of scientific investigation. But such empathy, Hempel argues, is neither necessary nor sufficient for establishing sound historical assessments. Not necessary, for we can establish laws for the behavior of people with whom we can have little empathy (psychotics, foreign cultures, etc.); not sufficient, for a strong feeling of empathy may very well accompany a completely mistaken assessment of another's actions (cf. Hempel 1949, pp. 467–468).

Objections to this theory are made from a variety of

points of view. One is to the effect that it presupposes what is to be proved, namely, that the historian's object in writing *is* to offer explanations and not a "deepening of [historical] consciousness"—in other words, "understanding"—which was Dilthey's contention (cf. Radnitzky 1968, II: 102). A more decisive objection, however, and one which attacks Hempel's position from methodological considerations, is that developed by William Dray, who argues, among other things, that there simply cannot be any Hempelian laws in historiography because the effort to specify such laws so that the antecedent circumstances could be subsumed under them would necessitate such a narrowing of the so-called general law that it would finally be a "law" with only one concrete application, and hence, in losing its general applicability, no law at all (see Dray 1957, pp. 33–39). Von Wright thinks Dray's critique of Hempel's theory decisive, though he is less sanguine about Dray's own theory, which rests rational explanation in history on the slippery footing of a logic of valuation.

Hempel's theory touches on hermeneutics in two ways. For one thing, its object is the historian's language rather than historical events or experiences themselves. For another, it rejects Dilthey's division of rational knowing into two categories, that of explanation and that of understanding; there can be only one form of rational explanation.

Though Hempel's theory was advanced only with regard to historiography, it is clear that it can be extended to other of the social sciences and perhaps even to such a field as aesthetics, if one tries to view that also as governed by psychological laws. In every case to explain rationally some phenomenon is to see that a set of circumstances grew to become the instantiation of a known lawlike relationship and hence that the event in question was bound, or bound with great probability, to occur. To "understand" the phenomenon in question can only mean something like this. Any other sense of understanding must refer to the private motions of sympathy or antipathy in an observer. These, however commonly present, are irrelevant to the rational status which some phenomenon or event has in our own or in the community's mind.

Among many English-language philosophers, Hempel's phrase "the method of empathic understanding" is accepted as a truncated but fair description of a philosophically oriented hermeneutics. Such an empathic hermeneutics is called psychologistic, because it is thought to suppose that an observer calls into play his own memories, impressions, or imagination of "what it's like" to be in a certain situation and on the basis of these to be able to experience an understanding of why this event occurred or was the way it was. This is sometimes called the "cup of coffee" view of hermeneutics, after the positivist philosopher Otto Neurath, who remarked in 1930 that such empathic understandings enter into the actual explanation or rational appreciation of an event about as much as does a good cup of coffee, which also awakens or at least sustains a researcher's mental powers.

The *locus classicus* attacking such a psychologistic hermeneutics is Th. Abel's 1948 article, "The Operation Called *Verstehen*" (Abel Th. 1953), where such "emotional syllogisms" are allowed at best to function as potential guides to or hypotheses about explanations, though they cannot enter into explanations in their own right. This psychologizing impression of hermeneutics persists today. It is restated, for example, in a current (1976) college textbook of introduction to philosophy:

> The term *verstehen* ('to understand') denotes the position of those who claim that the social scientist can and must make use of his own inner experience. . . . He must use the methods of *introspection* and *empathy,* which have nothing in common with the procedures of natural science. [R. Abel 1976, p. 108]

But, however common such psychologizing forms of understanding may be in our everyday lives and however much historical ground there may be for such interpretations of hermeneutics in its earlier advocates, it is clearly a fact that today's proponents of a methodology of understanding and of a fresh version of hermeneutics are *not* advocating some psychologistic sense of understanding. What they are advocating it will be the purpose of the rest of this book to expound, but it is important that empiricists wishing to reduce understanding to some form of explanation modeled on the methods of the natural sciences enter into discussion with *current* forms of hermeneutics and cease bothering with "earlier and outmoded versions of the methodology of empathy" (von Wright 1971, pp. 30–31).

The modern hermeneuticist, however, must recognize in his turn that empiricist theories of explanation

for the social sciences have developed far beyond that
advanced by Hempel in 1942. Though logical positivism has ceased to exist as a cohesive school, as mentioned earlier, its legacy continues in the orientation
loosely identified as logical empiricism, which may be
said to be an epistemology carried on in the "spirit of
positivism." The last phrase is cited from von Wright,
who writes:

> But it is true to say that the contributions of analytical
> philosophy to methodology and philosophy of science
> have, until recently, been predominantly in the spirit of
> positivism, if by "positivism" one understands a philoso-
> phy advocating methodological monism, mathematical
> ideals of perfection, and a subsumption-theoretic view of
> scientific explanation. [von Wright 1971, p. 9]

The thesis of methodological monism, that the
methodologies appropriate to the cultural and natural
worlds are essentially one, is a characteristic of the sort
of empiricism opposed by modern hermeneutics. The
thesis is a commonplace among logical empiricists.
One can see its recommended status in May Brodbeck's recent edition of articles on the philosophy of
the social sciences:

> If we grant the principle that the social disciplines are (or,
> more realistically, *can be*) sciences, then the philosophical
> problems of social science are those of all science. . . . That
> the answers to these and related questions are essentially the
> same, whether we are studying the stars or mice or men, is a
> vindication of that eighteenth-century [Enlightenment] vi-
> sion. [Brodbeck 1968, pp. 1–2]

The first thing to remark, therefore, in an effort to clarify the use of the family of terms "hermeneutics," "hermeneutical," and so on, as well as the use of the term "understanding-theory" and their cognates as they appear in this book is that modern hermeneutical theories of understanding oppose the monomethodological thesis often found in empiricist writings, and in particular the version which holds that all explanations are causalist in form. This characterization of modern hermeneutics is, admittedly, only negative and leaves too vague an impression. Some positive specification can now be indicated and developed further in the body of the work.

There is an analytic wing in the movement against monomethodologism and against the reduction of all explanation or understanding to causalist patterns. It is inspired especially by the work of the later Wittgenstein. Its adherents seem to find their geography of preference in a belt that runs from Scandinavia, across England, Canada, and the United States, and into Australia and New Zealand. There is also a phenomenologically inspired alternative to monomethodologism and "universal causation" (so to call it), basically dialectical and Hegelian in character, and worked out sometimes in a Marxist way and sometimes in a Husserlian or Heideggerian way. Here the geography of preference is clearly West Germany, the Netherlands, France, Belgium, and Italy. What is common to the analytic and phenomenological versions of contemporary hermeneutics is, besides their aversion to monomethodologism, the contention that intentionality and purpose are noetic and not merely psychological categories. In fact, it would not be too much to say that contemporary hermeneutics sets the positivist thesis on its head. Far from making the causalist sciences, such as physics, the models of rationality—with the consequence that purposefulness and value-judging become emotional and irrelevant appendages to rationality—hermeneutic philosophy in some ways makes intentional or non-causalist uses of language— its "living" usage, to recall Dilthey's categories—the fundamental and primordial use that makes even causalist explanations possible, in fact. To convey how this insight can be worked out will be the task of the rest of this book.

It is not easy to decide on a strategy for this task. Any fresh movement in philosophy is bound to experience ambiguity, false starts, misplaced emphases, tentative forays and, of course, plain mistakes, as well as some clear successes. What one finds, given a chance to view the movement from a sufficient distance, is a kind of curve or tree developing in a certain way. It is this general topography I am trying to describe in this book. I have limited myself to an exposition of a short list of hermeneutical philosophers who, all the same, have the virtue of being recognized as seminal thinkers in their field. As substantive (if far from exhaustive) examples of analytic hermeneutics I have chosen the Finnish philosopher, logician, and editor of Wittgenstein, Georg Henrik von Wright, and also the British philosopher Peter Winch.

The Continental wing of the movement is represented by the Frankfurt philosopher Jürgen Habermas, for a Marxist version of hermeneutics, and by the Heidelberg philosopher Hans-Georg Gadamer, for a Heideggerian version. (The French philosopher Paul

Ricoeur will appear briefly in the Conclusion to the book.)

The positions of these philosophers have curious cross-cultural affinities. Von Wright and Habermas, for example, however different otherwise, retain for science a certain normative role and stress method in their analyses. Their thought is noticeably antimetaphysical. Winch and Gadamer, on the other hand, though different in inspiration, meet in a certain skepticism about the virtues of methodology and are more open to a concept of truth that escapes the nets of rigorous science, at least if "rigorous" be thought of as synonymous with "exact." These cross-currents, as I have suggested, are hints that the curtain between Anglo-Saxon and Continental schools of philosophy may be dissolving here and there and beginning to let useful light through.

1

Analytic Hermeneutics

Something should be said to clarify the term *analytic* in the title of this chapter. Nothing peculiarly Kantian or sectarian is meant by it, nor is there some implicit reference to the term's long and still vigorous history (see Hintikka 1973, pp. 123–149 and also 199–221). The term is used here in the loose but pertinent characterization that van Heijenoort applied to Frege's work when he wrote, "Frege's philosophy is analytic, in the sense that logic has a constant control over his philosophical investigations; this marked a sharp break with the past, especially in Germany, and Frege influenced philosophers as different as Russell, Wittgenstein, and Austin" (van Heijenoort 1967, p. 324).

Frege's "sharp break" was with the metaphysical and psychological traditions then so prominent in Continental philosophy. He sought no transcendentalism of the sorts found in Kant or Hegel, nor even an epistemology of the sort found in Descartes, Hume, or Mill. Frege's genius was to discover the form of a new logic, a *lingua characterica* he called it, which was not merely a device for calculating—as old logic had been—but a genuine language with the special capacity of characterizing the relationships of all properties and objects in the universe. To see the universe in terms of the articulation of this language was to have in effect an analysis of reality and therefore to have to some degree an analysis of the conditions of truth. Frege's discovery of modern logic seemed to attain the goals aimed at by earlier metaphysical and epistemological traditions, but did so without having to appeal to such dubious entities as transcendental egos or absolute minds and without having to call on such mysterious psychological processes as Humean impressions or Millean associations. This new logic was public and apparently precise, philosophically neutral, and complete.

No wonder then that a considerable range of modern philosophy has been won over by Frege's "sharp break" with the past and has continued to honor Frege's basic insight that current progress will most quickly and securely be made in philosophy if we give logic, and not metaphysics or psychology, a "constant control" over our investigations. The most noticeable difference between current philosophizing and Frege's work is the introduction of an aspect of logic not known in Frege's day: semantics—that is, a logic not merely of non-defined variables plus constants but of propositional elements that have meaning in their own right.

Modern philosophy works semantically in both a formal way—as, for example, when semantical theory is itself the object of study—and a very informal way—that is, within the flesh-and-bone exchanges of ordinary language. The former, obviously, exists for the sake of the latter, and the latter just as obviously must in some way presuppose the former. It is not surprising, therefore, to find analytic philosophers moving fairly constantly between the two levels of reflection.

It is a typical feature of the style of philosophizing which stems from Frege that one begins with the acceptance of some bit or expression of knowledge or of some mental attitude as a given for discussion. With this in place as an accepted focus in a universe of discourse one tries to expose the conceptual map that permeates this universe, hoping to reveal the otherwise hidden logical lines of force. This type of analysis may reveal the need for a revision of our naive understanding of the logical network. It may suggest a subarea where a special kind of logic needs to be developed.

The type of Continental philosophizing which we will meet in subsequent chapters, however, is different. Its inclination is to raise about some isolated bit of knowledge or mental attitude a genetic question: not 'What is the logical pattern of this given?' but 'How did this given come about?' or 'What are the conditions necessary for its appearance?'

At the risk of over-simplifying excessively the differences in analytic and Continental styles of philosophy, one could say that the analytic philosophers ask about the necessary logical, and the Continental ones ask about the necessary ontological, conditions for the object under discussion (cf. Bubner 1976, pp. 59–77; Hintikka 1973, pp. 98–122; Føllesdal 1972, pp. 417–429). The risk in using labels like this lies in abetting a misapprehension already prevalent among some outside the analytic orientation: namely the notion that analytic philosophers study merely language and language-games, while the Continental philosophers study reality. This notion is mistaken. Wittgenstein's "language-game" is not a game of language merely but a game of life—or better, a "form of life"—which is played out in (among other areas) language. As Hintikka expresses it, "Language-games are not games *in* language, they are typically games played *by means of language*" (Hintikka 1976, p. 114). Writes Wittgenstein, "it is our *acting,* which lies at the bottom of the language-game" (Wittgenstein 1969, #204; cf. #110, #229). The analysis of language practiced, then, by the analytic philosopher is an analysis of the lived world, not merely of the grammatical one.

Still, the analysis one attempts can proceed in a distinctly "logicizing" way or not. The reader easily notices that analytic philosophers turn constantly for their inspiration to the modern masters of logical achievement. The Continental philosophers we will meet are just as dedicated to the classic masters such as Aristotle, Kant, Hegel, Marx, and Heidegger.

To summarize, the addition of 'analytic' to 'hermeneutics' in the title of this chapter is meant to indicate a preference for formal or logicist ways of elucidating the problems of intersubjective understanding. There is an enormous variation in ways of doing this. Key studies have come from Anscombe on the logic of intention, from Taylor and Kenny on the nature and explanatory role of the practical syllogism, from Danto and Davidson on the logic of action, and from von Wright and Hintikka on the development of special logics for the problems raised by the concept of action. Behind most of these efforts lies the seminal work of Wittgenstein.

It was necessary to choose from the wealth of studies available; this chapter singles out certain works of von Wright and of Winch as representative of an analytic hermeneutics. Why these two? Not for the reason, certainly, that they are thought to summarize or condense the work of others. The reason, rather, is partly taxonomic, in that von Wright explicitly enrolls himself in a hermeneutical orientation and also because Winch is thought by Continental hermeneuticists to be making contributions in their direction. The reason is also partly speculative, in that von Wright and Winch have fairly comprehensive positions to advance. Their work has large and immediate implications for some of the most persistent and interesting of philosophy's traditional concerns—freedom and determinism, for example, or relativism and absolutism, or the connection between thinking and acting. This immediate relevance to such traditional problems is a point that Continental philosophers also stress in their own work.

After this minipreface to chapter one, we may begin with a review of von Wright's thesis.

We recall that Dilthey's characterization of the cultural world depended on a feeling we have of interconnectedness between our own psyche and something outside us. In this perspective the criterion of distinguishing the cultural from the natural world—for distinguishing phenomena for understanding from those for explaining—was an internal, introspective one. Such a perspective sits ill both with modern science and with modern philosophy.

What has happened now is that the world—
"reality"—is seen as possessing two large process-categories, which may be roughly distinguished as the
worlds of "happening" and of "acting." Stars explod-
ing, humans breathing, and birds building nests belong to the former. People convening to write a constitution, to put on a play, and possibly to build houses
belong to the latter. The earlier, internal criterion of
feeling has vanished in favor of the external manifestation. The analytic philosopher wants to know what is
the logic, and thereby the true picture, of such manifestations. In particular, he wants to know whether the
logics for the process-categories of "happening" and
of "acting" will be essentially the same.

Consider, for example, the difference between
breathing and writing a check. The former may be
called an automatic activity carried on without conscious monitoring. The latter supposes, on the contrary, a network of conventions for its existence—a
network which, just because it is a conventional and
not a natural system, is in place only because some
people continue to want it there, not because there is
some parahuman force requiring it to be there. There
is, consequently, purposiveness in the activity of writing a check, a note of satisfying wants, of intentionality, and of aiming at something. This activity appears
to be a manifestation not only of an intention on the
part of the check writer but also of an intentionality
resident in the cultural network that wants there to be
such a system for debt-paying, and so on. Without
saying that the world of human behavior is in every
case purposive or intentional, it seems clear that a great
deal of it has the air of being goal-directed. This por-

tion of human activity is the traditional province of moral philosophy; and it is for his reflections in this area that Professor von Wright is best known.

In an early work, von Wright remarked that moral philosophy embraces three interrelated areas: the normative ('What should I do?'), the axiological ('Why should I do it?'), and the anthropological ('Are one's motives, wants, abilities, or intentions relevant to moral doing?'). Of these three the last is the most important: "The basis of ethics or philosophy of morals must be an anthropology or philosophy of man" (von Wright 1963a, p. 8).

How should one study these areas? In von Wright's view, formal study has been neglected, probably because so many recent philosophers have thought the areas of norm and value to be alogical. His own effort has been to remedy this lack. His 1963 books—*Norm and Action: A Logical Enquiry* and *The Logic of Preference*—are formal studies, in the main, of normative and axiological foci in moral philosophy. His writings in the 1970s—in particular *Explanation and Understanding* and *Causality and Determinism* (hereafter *EU* and *CD*)—are investigations into the anthropological field.

All these studies suppose and argue to some extent the inadequacy of traditional logic for the fields under discussion. As von Wright puts his general problem:

We could say that formal logic, as we know it today, is essentially the logic of a *static* world. Its basic objects are possible states of affairs and their analysis by means of such categories as thing, property, and relation. There is no room for *change* in this world. Propositions are treated as

definitely true *or* false—not as now true, now false. Things
are viewed as having or lacking given properties and not as
changing from, say, red to not-red.

Acts, however, are essentially connected with changes. A
state which is not there may come into being as a result of
human interference with the world; or a state which is there
may be made to vanish. Action can also continue states of
affairs which would otherwise disappear, or suppress states
which would otherwise come into being. A necessary requirement of a Logic of Action is therefore a Logic of
Change. [von Wright 1963*b*, p. vii]

In his earlier work, von Wright proposed a special
branch of modal logic for this purpose. This branch
came to be designated "deontic logic" (cf. Hilpinen
1971). Several researchers, however (von Wright included), were troubled by the lack of symmetry between basic modal patterns and deontic ones. For example, the statement 'If x is necessarily the case, then x
is the case' would be a theorem in modal logic but 'If x
ought to be the case, then x is the case' is not a theorem
in deontic logic. Such an example suggests that the
problems of moral philosophy cannot be satisfactorily
mapped simply by a special branch of modal logic.
Since the early 1970s, therefore, von Wright has proposed a different way of handling these problems,
with an approach based on a theory of necessary and
sufficient conditionship. This is inherently a simpler
logical apparatus, which one can see displayed to its
best advantage in both *EU* and *CD*. Von Wright
thinks this approach not only sound but far-ranging in
its implications: "A prospect is opened up for a solution to many difficulties of a logical and philosophical

nature associated with the very idea of a 'logic of norms'" (von Wright, in Hilpinen 1971, p. 160).

Georg Henrik von Wright

Von Wright's *Explanation and Understanding* is a subtle and compact work. The more recent *Causality and Determinism* is a restatement of its causation portion. It is likely that von Wright will offer a similar restatement of the intention portions of *EU*. The general lines of his argument are clear, though their exposition is complex and tightly interlaced.

1. He starts with a given: causalist procedures in the natural sciences.

2. He proposes logical and ontological frames for discussing the given.

3. The first part of his argument maintains that the viability of causalist procedures rests conceptually (logically) upon the viability of a concept of action. If the argument of this stage can be sustained it "shatters the positivist conception of law" (*EU*, p. 22).

4. The second phase of his thesis maintains that an analysis of action argues the viability of teleological explanation as different from causalist explanations. If the argument here can be sustained it restricts considerably the range of validity of Hempel's subsumption theory of explanation.

5. In his concluding chapter he applies these analyses to the work of the historian.

As one can see, the overall thrust of von Wright's argument is to unite rather than to divide the natural

and cultural sciences, but he does not do so in a way
that collapses their differences. On the contrary, he
validates in a fundamental way the differences already
evident in the history of science between the "Galilean" and "Aristotelian" traditions—the former typically espousing explanations of a causalist, the latter of
a teleological kind (see *EU,* Chap. I). We may say, if
von Wright's views can be sustained, that he fulfills the
long-range goal of Dilthey, to demonstrate comple-
mentary objectivities for the natural and historical sciences.

   Let us take up these points in turn.

   1. Science's dependence on the apprehension of systematic regularities is too obvious to need argument.
Whether and to what extent this apprehension involves *causal* regularities is more controversial.
Bertrand Russell thought causal language a nostalgic
but debilitating superstition among philosophers, "a
relic of a by-gone age, surviving, like the monarchy,
only because it is erroneously supposed to do no
harm" (cited in *EU,* p. 35). He proposes instead a
language of function and probability. Von Wright
agrees that such ideas as 'cause,' 'effect,' and 'causal
law' are hardly logical primitives. They are certainly
far from being unproblematic. It is a fact nevertheless
that these notions continue to appear prominently in
the interpretations that scientists give of their theories
and in accounts they offer of their experiments. Even if
scientists speak in terms of functional or probabilistic
relations, the ways they go about establishing these are
"normally highly typical of the way in which we acquire true causal knowledge, namely though experi-

mental interference with nature" (*CD*, p. 70; cf. *CD*, pp. 3–4 and *EU*, pp. 36–37). The current evidence, then, is against the supposition that causalist procedures and language can be exorcised from science. One reason for discussing them, in short, is that the topic is unavoidable.

There is another reason. Causalist procedures have been and still are often used as normative models in discussing such traditional philosophical problems as freedom and determinism, knowledge and opinion, contingency and necessity, and so on. Philosophy often shapes these discussions against the background of what it has presumed a scientific explanation to look like. The elucidation, consequently, of scientific explanation is of considerable interest to certain questions traditional in philosophy. "One of my aims here," remarks von Wright, "is to show that this concept of causation is subject to certain inherent limitations" (*CD*, p. 1).

We should pause to note the precision of von Wright's starting point. He is not embarking on the general problem of the "understanding of understanding." His question is narrower. He is concerned initially with understanding (knowing, explaining) within the natural sciences and even there only within a limited (causalist) phase of its operations—which he does not hold to be the only way science works. From there he moves to a consideration of the historical sciences. He stands apart, in this, from Dilthey and from some of the later hermeneuticists we will meet. He reminds us of Spinoza noting a certain puzzle that appears in our "reading" of reality and pausing to see

what a solution of this puzzle might look like and to
what it might lead, for the general interest of philosophy.

2. The logic proposed by von Wright is a familiar
two-valued propositional logic with tense modifiers.
The main requirement of the logic is that it allow us to
distinguish a species of causal connection from other
types of connection. The reason is that it is at least a
plausible suggestion—and not a possibility, therefore,
to be foreclosed—that causal connections state not
only 'Whenever p, then q' but also the counterfactual
element "Even when p wasn't there, q would have
been there had p been there." An extensionalist version
of logic does not allow, von Wright argues, the generation of this species of counterfactual. He therefore
chooses an intensionalist version of logic (cf. *CD,* pp.
8–9; *EU,* pp. 18–22).

Within this language, von Wright proposes the concepts of sufficient and necessary conditions as the expressions that "unpack" the notion of causation. He
thinks this approach promising and registers his sur-
prise that it has not been used by more philosophers.

Roughly put, a *sufficient* condition expresses the idea
that, in a given sequence p, q, an appearance of p guarantees the concomitant or future appearance of q (if p,
then q); a *necessary* condition says that the appearance
of q guarantees the concomitant or previous appearance of p (q only if p). The two are not the same and
knowledge of one neither implies nor excludes knowledge of the other. For example, one may think that the
atmospheric conditions of certain caves in France are
necessary for the production of Roquefort cheese without knowing what causes are sufficient for its produc-

tion. Or, one may know that tension is *sufficient* to cause a headache without knowing what conditions are necessary for that result (aside from trivial ones, such as having a head).

Scientific explanations are answers to Why-questions. These two conditions offer us two ways of answering such questions. Answers in terms of sufficient conditions tell us what events are bound to happen. They figure prominently in explanations of the predictability type. Answers in terms of necessary conditions tell us how an event was possible. They figure prominently in explanations of the retrodictive type— in geology, for example, or in the theory of evolution. Some patterns of explanation, peculiarly dependent on necessary conditions, cannot be used for predicting new occurrences. Von Wright remarks that it is "a mistake to think that a causal explanation, or a scientific explanation generally, is necessarily equivalent to a mechanism for predicting the phenomena explained; yet this mistake is not infrequently made" (*EU*, p. 58).

Von Wright also proposes an ontological frame. The *p*'s and *q*'s of the normal language stand for "states-of-affairs" in the world—such as that the sun is shining, the door is open, rain is falling, and the like. Their articulation in the modal language allows us to express sequences among them—a "history" of the world. Transitions between states-of-affairs or the continuance of a state of affairs over a time-span are "events." A set of connected transitions constitutes a "system" which is thus a fragment of the world's history. The states-of-affairs ingredient in systems are the building-blocks of the world. They are logically independent of each other (they may occur or fail to occur in any combination); and they are "generic"—that is, they may obtain or not obtain repeatedly (cf. *EU,* pp. 43–44; *CD,* pp. 13–17).

As one can see, this is in large part the *Tractatus*-world of the early Wittgenstein. *Is* the world a *Tractatus*-world? Von Wright confesses that he does not know. He adopts this world-space and the logical frame of his formal language as methodological devices for his discussion. But he observes, ". . . it is an undeniable fact that as a simplified model of a world, Wittgenstein's conception in the *Tractatus* is both interesting in itself and useful as a tool for a great many purposes in the philosophy of logic and of science" (*EU,* pp. 44–45). The adoption of this model authorizes his note that he is discussing facts and not, he seems to be warning, language (cf. *EU,* p. 184 n. 12).

Using this model and the earlier concept of system we can draw an oversimplified picture of a sequence of states in the world. Suppose it has three moments—an *A*-moment, a *B*-moment, and a *C*-moment. The picture could look like this:

$$A \text{———} B \text{———} C$$

A is a sufficient condition of *B* and *B* is a sufficient condition of *C*. This is a picture of a causalist system in the Humean sense. Universalized, it is a picture of a determinist history, in one widely accepted sense of determinism.

Or, the picture could look like this:

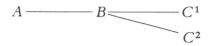

A is a sufficient condition of B but B may be only a necessary condition of the C-moment, with alternative developments possible in the system. Universalized, this would be a picture of history as a mixture of determined and (relatively) undetermined developments. A strict determinist would say of this second schema that the line between B and C^2 should really be dotted, to indicate that though we may (in our ignorance) *think* C^2 a genuine possibility, in reality it is not. But this is the place to note von Wright's caution that such questions are not to be decided by logic; only inquiry into experience can given us their answer.

3. He then advances to the construction of his thesis

My argument, to put it in a nutshell, will be this: The idea that causal connections are necessary connections in nature is rooted in the idea that there are agents who can interfere with the natural course of events. The concept of causation under investigation is therefore secondary to the concept of human action. [*CD,* p. 12]

The inquiry concerns the instantiation of a causality system in the world. How could we verify this? It involves our isolating the system from other systems, "closing" the system under investigation. There are several senses in which a system may be said to be "closed." Von Wright chooses this one: "no state (or feature of a state) at any stage in the system has an *antecedent sufficient condition* occurring outside the system" (*EU,* p. 54). What does it take to close a system in this way?

Suppose a doctor wishes to treat a patient with an allergic rash. The pathological condition is a small system in the patient's life history. Its endstate, the rash, is given, and closes the system on that side. The doctor needs to find the initial state, the cause that sets the system in motion. We realize that he must close the system on the near side if his treatment is to be effective. He may also need to characterize the inner articulation of the system. He may, for example, want to know that, though animal fur sets the system in motion, a high level of humidity prevents its worst effects. We know how he proceeds. He produces and withdraws certain elements in the environment presumed to be the initial causes setting the system in motion. If these manipulations succeed he has what he is looking for. If, after repeated tries, they do not—in other words, if he cannot find the initial cause on the other side of which does not lie still another sufficient condition concealed—he gives up the search for explanation and advises the patient to fall back on courage or prayer. In any case, it is only through his acting on the environment that he can close the system and so prescribe effective treatment. "In the idea of putting systems in motion," says von Wright, "the notions of action and causation meet" (*EU,* p. 64).

What is the logic of their meeting?

Let us review the doctor's case somewhat more abstractly. Let us suppose the doctor has found that animal fur sets the pathological system in motion. Is this enough? No, for synthetic fibers may also be setting the system in motion. Unless the doctor excludes this hypothesis, his telling the patient to stay away from animals will not be enough to cure the condition. Thus, the doctor's final answer (supposing he has an answer) that *p* (animal fur) produces *q* (rash) also entails his knowing that *r* (synthetic fabric) does not have this effect. The only logical formulation which could express the tie between *p* and *q* and at the same time exclude the possibility of *r* as a sufficient condition is one like this: On the occasions when *p* was not there *q* was not there either (even if *r* was), *but q would have been there had p been there*. It is this last, italicized portion that marks the closure of the system to the sufficient condition of *r,* so it is this portion that marks the tie between *p* and *q* as necessary. But this last portion is a counterfactual conditional. It follows that the truth of the doctor's explanation entails the truth of a counterfactual conditional.

What is involved in coming to know the truth of such a counterfactual conditional? It entails that the doctor can suppress *p* (animal fur) on occasions when it is there to see whether *q* then fails to appear; or to reproduce *p* on occasions when *p* is not there to see whether *q,* which also wasn't there, then shows up. In short, it conceptually entails his ability to interfere in the world.

But conception of an ability to interfere in the world is a conception of action.

Therefore, the conception of causation as the basis for asserting a nomic tie within the elements of a system supposes a conception of action.

An objection can be mounted against this argument.

It is important to see where the objection takes hold. It springs from a Humean conception of causality. The objection admits that the sequence 'p implies q' expresses a universal connection and, of course, that its truth rests on something other than logical necessity. It also admits that the experimenter is involved in establishing the truth of this connection, though it might consider "attention" a better word than "action" for describing his fundamental role. The objection is that passive observation is all that is needed for the experimenter to establish the non-logical necessity manifest in q's following upon p. Of course, experimenters do as a matter of fact typically "interfere" in nature where they can, setting systems in motion; but, the objection insists, the possibility of an effective interference of this kind is something that man learns from observation of regular sequences in nature. An example might be this: Man has observed in nature that warmth and light cause leaves to sprout and turn green. So, even in winter, he puts plants in greenhouses to force their blooming. It is, therefore, his observation of developing systems in nature that teaches man the possibilities of action; it is not action that teaches him the possibilities of natural systems (cf. *CD*, pp. 51–52).

The objection, answers von Wright, begs the question. It is at least conceivable, to refer to the above example, that some as yet unrecognized gas molecule in the air, perhaps not even generated by light, causes the reaction that makes leaves turn green. If we could discover it and manufacture it we could grow green vegetables even in the dark. The connection between light and greenness in leaves may in reality be accidental, not necessary. The objector has to admit this if the universality of the connection is to express a necessity which is other than logical necessity—where, say, the green leaves would be *defined* in terms of light.

But then, either we have submitted this "accidental" hypothesis to the test or we have not. If we have not, we have no way of deciding against that "accidental" possibility. If we have, and if the tests are successful, we have excluded that "accidental" hypothesis. Consequently, passive observation will not suffice for the establishing of a necessary but nonlogical tie in natural systems (cf. *EU,* p 71; *CD,* pp. 52–54).

It is, however, also important to see exactly where von Wright's answer takes hold. His argument here is not making an inductive or empirical statement to the effect that in our actual living we learn the possibilities of action before we learn the possibilities of nature. Whether this is so or not he does not know and doubts in any case whether it can be proved (cf. *EU,* p. 74). His argument at this stage is conceptual, not inductive: "the *concept* of causal connection rests upon the *concept* of action" (CD, p. 53). In fact, von Wright admits that "in the last resort, the notion of action is rooted in our familiarity with empirical regularities" (*EU,* p. 191 n. 41), but this admission, far from being a concession to his objector, is in fact an affirmation of the heart of his overall thesis. We had better pause to make the point clear.

We have, in the general pool of our experience, naive impressions of regularities in nature—some of them not in our power (such as the cycle of the seasons), and some of them initiated, we think, by ourselves (such as boiling water in preparation for making a cup of coffee). It is from this pool that we induce the idea that systems can be set in motion: "So, in the last resort the notion of action is rooted in our familiarity with empirical regularities." Familiarity, however, with causalist regularities is not the same thing as knowing the truth of them, since the regularity might be accidental, like the connection between the white color of swans and their species. To exclude this "accidentality" we call on that other realm of our naive impression of regularity, the one where we think we set systems in motion. Without this naive resource man "would simply not be familiar with the notion of counterfactuality, with the idea of *how it would have been, if* _____. *This* is the ground," continues von Wright, "for saying that the *concept* of causal connection rests on the *concept* of action" (*CD,* p. 53).

This thesis has an added advantage over Hume's. It respects our impression of the asymmetry of causation—rains cause floods, but we are not inclined to think that floods cause rain—without resting the essence of causality on temporal priority, as Hume's does—a thesis which von Wright thinks is open to serious objection in its own right (cf. *EU,* pp. 43, 74–81). His own position offers a way of distinguishing cause from effect in terms of the asymmetry of action, which may or may not involve temporal priority:

p is a cause relative to q, and q an effect relative to p, if and only if by doing p we could bring about q or by suppressing p we could remove q or prevent it from happening. In the first case the cause-factor is a sufficient, in the second it is a necessary condition for the effect-factor. [*EU,* p. 70]

And, as we have said, this thesis moves squarely against a positivist conception of law, for which universality and not necessity is the hallmark of nomic connection.

The thesis does not, of course, deny that causal sequences function nicely without our intervening. But it does mean that we cannot raise impressions of these sequences to the status of knowledge of causal laws without our active interference in the processes of nature. In calling on our familiarity with action von Wright rests his thesis, it is true, upon something mentalistic or "subjective," if one wishes to put it that way, in the notion of action. He admits that his view of action has a Kantian ring to it, that it resembles "a noumenal idea" (*EU*, p. 199 n. 36). But it is not psychologistic in the way Hume's thesis has often been thought to be. And it is based on a foundation in "facts of nature" (*CD*, p. 54). In sum, our "naive" impression of causalist regularities in nature leads to this very un-naive conclusion: "[To] think of a relation between events as causal is to think of it under the aspect of (possible) action. . . . For *that p* is the cause of *q*, I have endeavored to say here, *means* that I could bring about *q*, if I could (so that) *p*" (*EU*, p. 74).

The thesis has a practical difficulty inherent in it which inevitably engenders some complexity in the stages of the argument still to come: "There simply is no way of verifying whether a counterfactual statement is ever true" (*CD*, p. 50). Nevertheless, by his manipulation of systems, the experimenter can come "very close" to such verification (*EU*, p. 71). This means that man's confidence in the regularity of causal systems need not be "a matter of repeated lucky obser-vations" (*EU,* p. 73). It means that "we can be as certain of the truth of causal laws as we can be of our abilities to do, and bring about, things" (ibid.).

We conclude this step by referring to von Wright's "nutshell" statement cited at its head. Those lines con-tinue as follows: "And this implies, as I shall try to show, that the idea of causal determinism, associated with this idea of causation, can claim validity only for limited portions of the world, and not for the world as totality" (*CD,* p. 2). In other words, far from being antithetical to the concept of freedom, the concept of causation in some way involves it. This is a conclusion of more than passing philosophical interest. It means that all efforts to establish universal determinism of a causalist sort—as opposed to establishing such deter-minism for fragments of the world—are inherently self-defeating. One must be outside the system in or-der to manipulate it, interfere with it—in short, to "close" it. But, to echo Wittgenstein's remark in the *Tractatus,* there is no way to step outside the world. The thesis also means that there is one fragmentary system that in principle can never be established as totally determined—the system of the researcher him-self. Perhaps the researcher, in his experimentation, "shows," one may say, what he cannot demonstrate. This too has echoes of the *Tractatus*-world, but it is a different version of Wittgenstein's insight.

4. In the second phase of his argument, von Wright proposes an analysis for the concept of action and asks what, if any, kind of explanation could be given for an event described as "actionist," or, as one more often says, "intentional."

As an event, an action is a transition between states-of-affairs (including doing nothing, which is "forbearance" from action) and is, therefore, empirical. This empirical aspect is its "outer" face. It has also an "inner" side—the will or intention "behind" the action. But this last is to be taken in an "unproblematic sense" (*EU,* p. 91). Von Wright thus skirts a difficulty Dilthey got himself into—the nature of inner life. Von Wright thinks he does not have to adopt a position on this. Putting the point in a rather roundabout way, the reason von Wright's thesis excludes doctrinaire behaviorism of the stimulus–response kind (a causalist behaviorism) lies, not in his assumption of some spiritual essence or soul, but in his rejection of a causalist explanation for all human action (cf. *EU,* p. 193 n. 8). Still, this "inner" side lurks behind the discussion as an inadequately explored aspect. Its persistence is, I think, the main reason von Wright calls his notion of action, "though not exactly in the Kantian sense, a noumenal idea."

Von Wright is not legislating *the* sense of our usage of the term *action*. He holds only that, for an important class of actions, to say that someone "acts" means that he has made something true which was not otherwise true. In this description there is an explicit reference to something the agent did (e.g., murdered a man) and an implicit reference to something that, without his intervention, would have been the case (the continuing life of that man). There is a close tie between the "explicit," "outer" face of the action and its "implicit," "inner" side: "The object of this implicit reference I shall call *the counterfactual* element involved in action" (*CD,* p. 39). If von Wright's thesis can be sustained, therefore, the counterfactual condition is a general logical form which has (at least) two kinds of instantiation, a causalist and an intentionalist kind. The difficulties inherent in the verification of counterfactual forms show up here, in the case of intentionality, in a more basic way.

Suppose, now, a person thinks he acts. For example, I put a coin into a machine. Various closures open, pipes spout, gears whir, and a cup of coffee appears in the window. I think the cup of coffee would not have appeared there without my acting. This "no coffee" is the implicit or counterfactual reference involved in my action. The appearance of the cup of coffee is part of the explicit reference of my action.

Let us distinguish three moments in this system: (1) the coin's falling into the slot, (2) the internal writhings of the machine, and (3) the appearance of the cup of coffee in the window. It is not of critical importance which of these be taken as the primary object or reference of my intention, though one of them is usually singled out. Let us single out moment (1). The coin's falling into the slot, then, is "intentional." This description now spreads itself over the succeeding states of the system. If challenged, I would say, "Well, yes, I intended moments (2) and (3) also."

Suppose someone wants to refute my description of moment (1) as intentional. What, first, is his position? He cannot mount a challenge from logic alone, for two reasons: a counterfactual condition cannot be proved inherently vicious and logic does not decide questions of fact. Nor can he mount his challenge from an empirical thesis of universal causalism, for, as step (3) of von Wright's argument proves, this thesis supposes what it needs to establish. The challenger has only empirical arguments to call on. He must take each case in turn. What could he say to make me give up my description of moment (1) as intentional?

Suppose he could prove to me that a diabolical psychologist (or a clever computer) is monitoring me secretly so that every time I brought a coin near the machine the sequence began and produced a cup of coffee. I might then retreat somewhat—perhaps altogether—from my intentional description, "shrink" the range of my intentional action. But I would probably still say, 'Well, I intended to do *something*.' "We sometimes make," von Wright observes, "such 're-tractive' moves in our descriptions of actions, but they are the exception and not the rule" (*EU,* p. 127).

In any case there are limits to this shrinking, one "absurdist," so to speak, at the extreme outer boundaries; the other logical, at the individual himself.

At its extreme outer boundaries—in other words, when the "shrinking"-thesis is pushed to universal application—we would have the situation in which people would give up the idea that they ever do anything and resign themselves to admitting, like some fatalists, that everything happens of its own accord. "There would be no sure way of disproving this hypothesis, but there are also no good grounds for believing it" (*EU,* pp. 127–128). And there are good grounds for disbelieving it, namely our relatively successful tests for causal counterfactuality; for the viability of these supposes a corresponding viability in our concept of action. (Imagine our doctor, mentioned earlier, saying to his patient, "Well, if you're going to get a rash, you're going to get a rash. If not, not." The patient might not be able to disprove this opinion, but he is not likely to think hearing it worth the fee.)

At its narrowest end the causality hypothesis is logically limited by the concept of 'basic actions'—that is, "actions which are performed directly and not by doing something else" (*EU,* p. 128). My moving my arm, with or without a further end in view, would be an example. Could someone prove to me that there is a genetic or cortical "computer" in me, making this movement come about by a string of sufficient conditions? *That* such a description be offered of an event is logically possible. It would, however, have to be offered by someone other than myself. What is excluded is that *I* both move my arm (do the action) and observe a cause moving it (make it happen): "It is a contradiction in terms both to let and to make the same thing happen on the same occasion" (*EU,* p. 130). But the possibility remains that both a causalist and an intentionalistic description can be offered for the same event in the world, though from different points of view. What von Wright wishes to stress is that the logic of the one does not imply or exclude the logic of the other: the relation between them is "contingent" (*CD,* p. 49).

The two limits together present us with a strange type of antinomy or asymmetry in the utility of self-reflection: at the universal level, it is logically possible that universal determinism be true, but the only steps that could make the thesis empirically verifiable are those that logically forbid its empirical verification; at the individual level, it is empirically (and, of course, logically) possible that the same behavior be given either a causalist or an intentionalist description, but it is logically impossible that the two compatible descriptions be established by the same researcher for the same event. Language may limit the way I see my world, as the *Tractatus* says, but it is equally certain that the characteristics of my world limit the applicability of language.

Let us grant that an event in the world resists a causalist description and may fairly be called intentional. We now want to explain this event. Can a causalist model of explanation do this?

The likely, though perhaps not the only, model to choose for consideration is the practical syllogism. This does not prejudge the issue. A practical syllogism may well be "only a disguised form of nomological–deductive explanation in accordance with the covering law model" (*EU,* p. 98). Many are. Can this be the case with an event *(explanandum)* described as intentional?

What is "practical" about this sort of inference is that the conclusion assented to is an action (or a statement describing an action), rather than a conception or belief, as would be the case for a theoretical syllogism. In a *causalist* explanation of such an inference, the descriptions of the states-of-affairs in the premises and conclusion must be, as was said earlier, logically independent of one another: the truth of one neither implies nor excludes the truth of the others. Can a causalist explanation for an intentional *explanandum* respect this requirement?

We have seen above that if causalistically described premises could account for the intentional event in the conclusion the subject would then say, 'Oh, I guess my "action" was not really an action after all.' The intentionality of the conclusion would disappear. By adapting von Wright's earlier statement we could say that there sometimes are such "retractive" explanations. How exceptional they are is open to debate. But it still remains true that we have no good grounds for believing that such causalistic explanatory moves are everywhere the case. It also remains true that the same occurrence in the world may submit to alternative explanations, causalistic or intentionalistic, though not in the same inferential schema. The relation of the two, if the argument of this last point can be established, would be "contingent": the explanatory schemata neither imply nor exclude each other.

So, let us take an inferential schema which is intentionalist. We use our earlier example.

1. *A* wanted a cup of coffee.

2. *A* thought it was necessary for this (and he hoped it was sufficient) to put a coin in the machine.

3. Therefore, *A* put a coin in the machine.

This schema presents an explanation, an answer to the question, 'Why did *A* put a coin in the machine?'

Two questions arise: Can such a teleological explanation exist? (No, if it is only a disguised causalistic explanation.) Can such an explanation be true? (Yes, if evidence can be found for its several statements.)

That a teleological explanation is not a disguised causalistic one can be proved by showing that the verification of its several statements mutually involve each other, thus violating the causalistic explanation's requirement that the verification of the several statements *not* mutually imply each other.

Consider step 3 of this inferential schema. What would be required to verify it as an intentionalistic description of an event? Noting sheer behavior will not do, since *A* might have acted in a reflex manner or under debilitating coercion, in a dream, under hypnosis, and so on. Nor will failure of performance show it, since intentions do not always succeed in coming to term. What is required to verify intentionalistic behavior is to show that it is "'aiming' at a certain achievement, *independently* of whether it accomplishes it or not" (*EU*, p. 109). But this aiming at is what is asserted in step 1. The verification of step 3, therefore, logically involves the verification of step 1.

Or, consider the description offered in step 2. Given the "inner" character of intentionality, we might try to verify step 2 by appealing to patterns in *A*'s culture, where certain apprehensions of relations between means and ends are prevalent. But *A* might deny that he shares those cultural notions, and he might be correct (cf. *EU*, pp. 111–112). Or, we could try it by appeal to *A*'s verbal reports. But *A* might be deceiving us (cf. *EU*, pp. 112–114). Finally, we could use *A*'s introspection. But such "inner" awareness of intentionality just is his intention and hence what he needs to establish (cf. *EU*, p. 114). In short, to verify step 2 we need external behavior (the "outer" face) of a certain type, an "aiming" type. But this is what is asserted in step 3. Verification of step 2, therefore, logically involves verification of step 3.

All this runs squarely against the schema of a causalistic explanation, which not only does not but must not suppose that, in order to verify whether a flood took place, I need to verify whether it rained.

Can evidence be offered for the (interdependent) truth of statements in a teleological schema? Clearly, yes. A combination of behavior observation, verbal reports, documents supporting these, reports of cultural attitudes, and the like form an interlocking web of evidence. This is precisely what the historian seeks. This effort to establish verification can never be more than a "very close" verification, because the historian is trying to prove the instantiation of a counterfactual element that is doubly evasive because it is the instantiation of a counterfactual that is intentionalistic rather than causalistic. But the reason for the historian's lack of success, if that is the result, will be contingent, not inevitable. The historian is not, as positivists have claimed, hopelessly on the wrong track.

We end this section with a comment on the nature of von Wright's contribution to the problem of understanding. The main thing we notice is that his solution to the problem invokes a syllogism, a discursive procedure. Intuition, except in a restricted sense to be explained in a moment, plays no part. His solution makes clear contact with the reasoning procedures already familiar in the natural sciences and is methodologically continuous with them. He does not call for a fundamental renewal of the philosophy of science. He trusts the procedures already practiced, though, as is obvious, he thinks a more careful use of semantic analysis shows that certain extravagances—such as those of positivism—are mistaken. Kant's question was "How is reliable knowledge possible?" Dilthey's question was "How is historical knowledge possible?" Von Wright's question is "How is historical knowledge scientifically respectable?"

Something else follows. Committed to a solution in terms of a syllogism, von Wright will have to suppose that the statements making up the syllogism, while they are empirical statements, describe generic features of events—that is, features that are in principle repeatable. The statements could not link together syllogistically otherwise. A solution, then, to the problem of universals is supposed, but von Wright does not discuss this.

This said, one is not surprised to learn that von Wright does not use such a phrase as "historical understanding," which one finds in Dilthey. He always says instead "historical explanation." Understanding is not explanation: it is the prelude to explanation. It is the interpretative act that sets up the object of explanation, the *explanandum,* the conclusion of the practical syllogism for which the appropriate premises must be found. He summarizes this point as follows:

Before explanation can begin, its object —the *explanandum*—must be described. Any description may be said to tell us what something "is." If we call every act of grasping what a certain thing is 'understanding,' then understanding is a prerequisite of every explanation, whether causal or teleological. This is trivial. But understanding what something is in the sense of *is like* should not be confused with understanding what something is in the sense of *means* or *signifies.* The first is a characteristic preliminary of causal, the second of teleological explanation. It is therefore misleading to say that understanding versus explanation marks the difference between the two types of scientific intelligibility. But one could say that the intentional or nonintentional character of their objects marks the difference between two types of understanding and of explanation. [*EU,* p. 135]

The description, then, of an event is the fundamental hermeneutical act. It steers any further elaboration in one direction or another. Here von Wright makes contact with a point of fundamental importance to contemporary Continental hermeneuticists—more noticeably so with Habermas (see the next chapter). Von Wright says that even for us to register an impression of causal regularity we accompany it with the idea of future "possible action." This holds true whether the regularity is one we can do something about (like a pathological condition) or one that we cannot (like the effects of the Ice Age on the survival of dinosaurs). Even causal behavior, therefore, has an implicit but conceptual reference to the interests we have in acting. Knowledge and interests are internally connected.

5. Finally, von Wright applies his analysis, so far confined to the actions of an individual, to the actions of groups. Nowhere, of course, has he denied that there is room also for explanation of a Humean kind in a total and adequate explanation of intentional behavior. It is especially obvious that causes of a Humean kind are at work in the events that historians and social scientists try to explain. But what interests the historian is not only or even chiefly the physical means that, say, an aggressor used to destroy a city, but the motivations that led to this destruction or the effects that the destruction had on the attitudes of the native population. Often a causal explanation highlights and suggests non-Humean antecedents and consequences; but it does not explain them.

Using as an example the sequence of events leading from the shots at Sarajevo to the outbreak of the First World War, von Wright shows that the adequate explanation uses a combination of causal and intentionalist explanations. Because of its typical combinatory form he calls such an explanation 'quasi-causal' (*EU,* p. 142).

One begins with a premise, established by other practical inferences, that the Austrian government wished to consolidate and extend its influence in the Balkans. Suppose it had the more or less settled opinion that *a* was a necessary and perhaps sufficient means to that end. But the shots at Sarajevo changed the situation. It was now no longer thought that *a* was necessary or sufficient but that *b* was now necessary (and maybe sufficient). Hence the Austrians did *b*, which was to deliver an ultimatum to Serbia. But this led the Russians to think that the mobilization of their army was necessary. From this the Serbians took heart and defied the ultimatum of the Austrians. The Austrians then considered it necessary to declare war on Serbia.

At each step certain actions created a new situation.

In this new situation a certain action *became* necessary which—the aims and ends of action being the same—had not been necessary before. One could say that the event, *viz.* the assassination, 'actuated' or 'released' a practical inference which was there 'latently.' The conclusion of the actuated inference, i.e. the issuing of the ultimatum, created another situation (on the part of the Russian cabinet) which again created a new situation (like the mobilization), actuating further practical inferences, the final 'conclusion' of which was the outbreak of the war. [*EU,* p. 143]

The linkage, then, from the assassination to the war was not one of pure sufficient conditions. The shots at

Sarajevo were sufficient (causalistically) to change drastically the states-of-affairs but not to dictate the meaning or significance which this change would have on the minds of the Austrians. The covering law model would wish to bypass this area of initiative in the position of the Austrian cabinet and appeal to a general law of some kind, one saying perhaps that 'Assassinations of heirs to the throne have as their consequence ultimata delivered by the aggrieved nation to the nation of the assassin.' Such a law is historically untrue and unlikely. "Would," asks von Wright, "[the Austrian cabinet] have issued a similar ultimatum to Denmark if the archduke on a pleasure trip to Greenland had been killed by a mad eskimo?" (*EU,* p. 140). If one replies that one needs to specify the circumstances much better than this, then one falls into the difficulty enunciated by Dray. In any case, "specify the circumstances" is a vague phrase for which von Wright is seeking some precision.

One can now see what von Wright means by calling the pattern of historical argument "quasi-causal"— that is, not purely intentionalist: the physical "events are linked . . . through practical syllogisms" (*EU,* p. 142). (This does not imply that the actors need consciously to formulate such syllogisms.) The fact of the assassination affects the premises of a practical inference (and this is not a disguised covering-law inference), which issues in a new fact (the ultimatum), which further affects the practical inferences of the Russians, which issues in a new fact (the decree of mobilization), and so on. Thus the linkage rests upon an impression of regularity which the Austrians *think,* given the circumstances, is true. If von Wright's argument in the previous sections is correct, then the regularity which they think is true is an intentionalistically engendered regularity. In other words, the system ("fragment of the world's history") is thought to contain at least one link which is considered necessary but is not presumed to be sufficient (though they hope it is sufficient). It is this "necessary" but not necessarily "sufficient" element in the ontology of systems which makes room for initiative, action, intentionality, the opportunity to make the world a little bit different from what it otherwise would be.

It may be true that a particular historian is selective in his search for these intentionalities. Sometimes this is due to the limited perspective available to him at the time of writing. (One does not expect historians to write the histories of revolutions in the same way before and after Marx, for example.) Or it may be due to less excusable sympathies which a historian has for some of the actors of history but not for others. But these sympathies, if they are to have fruitful issue, are sympathies for the actors' practical inferences, not for the actors' own irrationalities. One may then grant that an element of subjectivity is there in the work of historians. Von Wright is far from denying it. But, all that said, it remains true that the *explanation* a historian offers for a sequence of events in history is one that can only be grounded "on *facts,* and not on what the historian *thinks* about them" (*EU,* p. 156).

But consider this last statement. We know what von Wright means. Historians' explanations are neither disguised covering-law schemata on the one hand nor exercises in psychologistic empathy on the other. Still, a mystery remains. Can "facts" account for what an agent (or a historian) thinks about them? We recall von Wright's insistence that verification of counterfactual elements can only come "close" to conclusive verification. And we appreciate that this is doubly difficult in the case of actionist counterfactuals. The situation leading up to the First World War is not in any unproblematic sense repeatable. Further, the records and documents from that period themselves survive partly from accident and partly from practical inferences which memoirists, archivists, and the like made concerning their "significance." We have not, then, the same opportunity of controlled assessment of facts as we do in the case of causalist counterfactuals. The question then arises, How to explain the "meaningful" impact that the "facts" had on the purposes of the actors, as well as that which the documents had on the assessment of the archivist (historian)? *That* they had an impact is granted, but can an explanation be offered for the meaning (the "aiming at" element) vested in them by the actors or historians? That such an explanation, if it could be offered, need not be of a causalist or Humean kind follows immediately from von Wright's argument. It is a considerable achievement to show this, and it removes at one stroke a whole false route which many contemporary methodologists in the social and historical sciences seem doggedly intent on following. But von Wright is also aware of what he has left undone. A pertinent passage, partially cited earlier, is worth quoting in full:

> The distinction which I have made between an outer and an inner aspect of action can, and should, be understood in an unproblematic sense. It does not prejudge the difficult

question of the nature of the "inner." There is, for example, no claim that it is a mental act or process or a state of mind or an "experience." We shall also try to bypass this problem as much as possible. But it will inevitably lurk in the background as soon as we raise the further question of how the two aspects of action [i.e., the "aiming-at" aspect and the physical "result"] are related. [*EU*, p. 91]

It turns out that they are conceptually or logically related. This relationship shows up, naively so to speak, in our "familiarity with empirical regularities"—including those of an actionist kind. It is given more precise formulation (and, at the same time, the "undone" aspect of von Wright's thesis is suggested) in the following passage:

The mere understanding of behavior as action, e.g. button-pressing, without attributing to it a remoter purpose, e.g. making a bell ring, for the attainment of which the action is a means, is itself a way of explaining behavior. Perhaps it could be called a rudimentary form of a teleological explanation. It is the step whereby we move the description of behavior on to the teleological level, one could say. But it seems to me clearer to separate this step from explanation proper, and thus to distinguish between the *understanding of behavior* (as action) and the *teleological explanation of action* (i.e., of intentionalistically understood behavior). [*EU*, p. 124]

But the former step, where understanding of behavior is itself intentionalistic, thus giving rise to a pool of familiarity with actionist regularities, is, for other hermeneuticists, *the* hermeneutical moment and the one that, above all others, needs to be clarified. We shall see, among the authors who follow, several different ways of attempting this clarification. One of them, Peter Winch, remains closely tied to the analytic tradition, and it is to the consideration of his thesis that we now turn.

Peter Winch

We should bear in mind that Winch's *Idea of a Social Science and Its Relation to Philosophy* (1958; hereafter *ISS*) was written much earlier than von Wright's *Explanation and Understanding*. A selection of Winch's articles, conveniently collected in *Ethics and Action* (1972; hereafter *EA*), also antedates *EU*. There is not a basic incompatibility in the two authors' views. Von Wright remarks, "One misses in Winch's book the aspect of intentionality and teleology" (*EU,* p. 29); but, if the last remarks about von Wright's approach are justified, Winch could make a similar remark about von Wright. Some passages in Winch's later articles sound very similar to what von Wright says. For example:

> But forms of life are, or involve, human activities, things that men do; or better, they provide a context within which we can make sense of the idea of men doing things, in that they enable us to speak of standards and criteria by reference to which human choices are made and understood: by reference to which, that is, we can see what it is for a man to have an alternative before him and to do one thing rather than another. [*EA,* p. 125]

In short, although it would be a category-mistake, in the area of the problem raised, to try to fuse into one the two perspectives of von Wright and Winch, their membership in the analytic family is plain.

What is implied, Winch wants to know, in our having those patterns which all understanding involves? His thesis is "that criteria of logic [as also of less formal modes of understanding] are not a direct gift of God, but arise out of, and are only intelligible in the context of, ways of living or modes of social life" (*ISS,* p. 100; cf. p. 126). It is a Kantian question, about the possibility of knowledge; but Winch does not find his answer in a Kantian self, logically pre-instructed, nor in a Diltheyan self, psychologically and ontologically interconnected with other selves. Human intercourse is not just the place where understanding surfaces (which Dilthey also said) but the fundamental source of its possibility.

Winch's thesis goes much further than Dilthey's Dilthey asked about the understanding of understanding where this last was, along with explanation, a subspecies of the more general class 'knowledge.' Winch collapses Dilthey's incipient parallelism. For him the foundations of the social sciences are the foundations for all intelligibility, whether in the natural or in the cultural sciences. Winch's thesis, in a way reminiscent of von Wright's, does not preclude the possibility of entertaining "an ideal of unified science," though this would certainly not take the form which positivism prescribes.

The generality of his question marks Winch's genuinely philosophical thrust: "Whereas the scientist investigates the nature, causes, and effects of *particular* real things and processes, the philosopher is concerned with the nature of reality as such and in general" (*ISS,*

8; cf. 102). This applies not just to science but to philosophy as well. Philosophy is not one among several diversified but cooperating ways of inquiry, with a special field staked out for its cultivation. To think so is to suppose the "master scientist" or "underlaborer" conception of philosophy, which Winch attacks in the earlier portions of his book. The particularities of puzzles investigated within these narrower perspectives do indeed require treatment, but the thread that runs through them all is the deeper one which Winch, quoting Burnet, expresses this way: "'. . . whether the mind of man can have any contact with reality at all, and, if it can, what difference this will make to his life'" (*ISS,* p. 9). Winch's question, therefore, is plainly epistemological, even in (as he remarks) an old-fashioned sense of the term.

But here Winch's argument takes a characteristically analytic turn. His generalism does not tempt him to the grand vision of such thinkers as Hegel, Marx, or Husserl. It is no more, he says, the commission of philosophy to provide one overarching set of criteria for intelligibility than it is to confine itself to piecemeal work: "Its task will rather be to describe the conditions which must be satisfied if there are to *be* any criteria of understanding at all" (*ISS,* p. 21). Where are these conditions whose description philosophy is to attempt? In the usages of language, Winch answers (following the later Wittgenstein): "In considering the nature of thought one is led also to consider the nature of language. Inseparably bound up with the question whether reality is intelligible, therefore, is the question of how language is connected with reality, of what it is to *say* something" (*ISS,* p. 2).

This is not to urge, as some others influenced by Wittgenstein have done, that problems of philosophy arise out of language "*rather than* out of the world," for the reason that "in discussing language philosophically we are in fact discussing *what counts as belonging to the world*" (*ISS,* p. 5). What are the necessary general conditions, then, which must be present in order for my language to refer to something, in order for my expressions to have meaning in that sense, to be able to "give" me a world?

To answer this it is necessary to see how experiences of intelligibility (and of nonintelligibility) involve general consideration of the activities of human society and involve, therefore, from a philosopher's perspective, "an analysis . . . of the concept of human society" (*ISS,* p. 23). The latter expression is slightly misleading, for it may suggest that the object of analysis is some sort of inner mental possession or that the method of analysis may be purely formal. In fact the object is what we agree to be meaningful behavior, "this actual flesh-and-blood intercourse" (*ISS,* p. 126) which "counts as" the experience of having a society. Hence, it is Winch's thesis, understanding occurs primitively as a "form of life" and as a social form of life.

An analysis of this given reveals two paradoxical implications.

One is that understanding cannot simply be learning to associate a certain sound with a certain thing, as perhaps a dog may (and as associationist theories of language-learning suppose). Two considerations show this. Understanding means "knowing how to go on," as for example in understanding an arithmetic technique; "it is learning *to do* something" (*ISS,* p. 57). So far, the associationist is not in disagreement. He simply attributes to this "learning" a purely behavioral content and would urge against Winch, "But couldn't the child learning his tables (or the meaning of a word) simply imitate his teacher and continue the progression of marks (or continue applying the sound to the thing) in the same way as the teacher was doing it?" (In the same spirit, "Doesn't the dog 'understand' 'Roll over' because he performs the same behavior each time on hearing that sound?") Winch answers, no. For the critical question is, "What counts as performing the *same* behavior?" Sameness of behavior can only be registered by one in a position to compare this behavior to a past or future behavior and to recognize in them an identity of form. It is the master, and not the dog, in whom resides this possibility of judgment of sameness in the dog's behavior. The dog's behavior "requires a reference to *human* activities, and norms which are here applied analogically to animals" (*ISS,* p. 60; cf. p. 65). The same essential point is true of the child's learning an arithmetic technique or of anyone's learning what a word means. In both cases, understanding the technique or the meaning of the word implies the ability to recognize sameness in other circumstances which call for application and sameness in the actual method of application. But this means that the understander is in possession of a rule that guides his "going on." (He need not have a conscious formulation of it; one most often speaks his native tongue intelligibly without an explicit awareness of its rules of grammar.) Hence, as Wittgenstein showed, the concepts 'rule' and 'same' are conceptually "interwoven" (*ISS*, p. 28; cf. Wittgenstein 1968, I: 225).

This introduces the other paradoxical feature of the exercise of understanding, that it excludes the possibility of there being an understanding that is, in principle, private.

"What is the difference," asks Winch, "between someone who is really applying a rule in what he does and someone who is not?" (*ISS*, p. 29). It is true that an observer, *O*, standing apart from a subject, *N*, can always find some rule to describe *N*'s behavior, even if *N* is behaving quite erratically. But this will not assure him that *N* is applying the rule. How can one know when he or another is applying a rule? The criterion is this: "it is only in a situation in which it makes sense to suppose that somebody else could in principle discover the rule which I am following that I can intelligibly be said to follow a rule at all" (*ISS*, p. 30); by "intelligibly be said" he means, by someone in a position of being able to say what would count as *not* following the rule, of being able to see what would count as a contravention of the rule (cf. *ISS*, p. 32). This does not imply, of course, that an observer has to be actually present in order for rule-following to take place. Robinson Crusoe could do it (or fail to do it) quite nicely alone. It only means that the behavior is in principle observable as an exercise in rule-following.

The above entails that all experience of understanding and of intelligibility, in the sense where 'understanding' means to understand what it means to be able to say something, involves a society as a form of life in which conventions are established for the senses of 'same' and 'rule-following.' In this way the analysis of understanding leads directly to the recognition of human society as the necessary condition which, like water for the fish's existence, makes understanding possible. Inasmuch as understanding is an apprehension of reality, it makes a world possible. Sociology, then, turns out to be linked with epistemology and ontology in a more general way than Dilthey, in his restricted concept of 'understanding,' allowed for "historical understanding." While it is true that sociologists search out the particular rule-following that goes on in regional groupings—among college students, in the military, among ethnic groups, and the like—each of these supposes an understanding, both in the researchers and among their subjects, of what rule-following includes. That is why, as Collingwood and Max Weber both pointed out, understanding another cannot be reduced to an empathic "feeling-with." It is not a question of feeling at all, but a question of knowing—namely, of knowing what it means to follow a rule and what different rule-followings look like. This fundamental supposition of sociology is conceptually, not psychologically, interwoven with epistemology: "In fact, not to put too fine a point on it, this part of sociology is really misbegotten epistemology. I say 'misbegotten' because its problems have been largely misconstrued, and therefore mishandled, as a species of scientific problem" (*ISS,* p. 43).

But, one may further add, this part of sociology is really misbegotten ontology as well. To refer to von Wright's example, when the Austrian cabinet learned of the assassination at Sarajevo, what they saw in that event was not just a physical variation in the total state of the world but a disruption in a web of internal relations which they thought (and wished) their society to have. To put it another way, purposiveness was not subsequent to that event and did not arise in the world after that event; it was already in the world and, in fact, was what gave that transition in states-of-affairs its event-ful character. The assassination, analogous to a violation of grammar in a language, violated a network of internal relations which constituted the Austrian world. Reality itself has a "meaningful configuration" to it, says Winch, citing Max Weber (*ISS,* p. 45). What distinguishes the "meaningful configuration" of reality from chaos is the presence in it of a commitment to the future. This holds true even for those events which are the subject of scientific investigation and causalist explanation. It is especially pertinent to the events the social scientist is interested in and steers toward a different kind of explanation. And it is normally in this sense that Winch uses the term 'meaning' (in fact, it is in this sense that Weber uses it in the quotation above). The idea is that the world's commitment to the future and the commitment of my actions to the future is "identical in form with the connection between a definition and the subsequent use of the word defined. . . . [This] is possible only where the act in question has a relation to a social context" (*ISS,* p. 50). It strikes us as strange that "social relations should be like logical relations between propositions," but perhaps our feelings of anomaly can be assuaged if we see that "logical relations between

propositions themselves depend on social relations between men" (*ISS*, p. 126). The passage here is worth
quoting at some length.

Part of the opposition one feels to the idea that men can be
related to each other through their actions in at all the same
kind of way as propositions can be related to each other is
probably due to an inadequate conception of what logical
relations between propositions themselves are. One is inclined to think of the laws of logic as forming a *given* rigid
structure to which men try, with greater or less (but never
complete) success, to make what they say in their actual
linguistic and social intercourse conform. One thinks of
propositions as something ethereal, which just because of
their ethereal, non-physical nature, can fit together more
tightly than can be conceived in the case of anything so
grossly material as flesh-and-blood men and their actions.
In a sense one is right in this; for to treat of logical relations
in a formal systematic way is to think at a very high level of
abstraction, at which all the anomalies, imperfections and
crudities which characterize men's actual intercourse with
each other in society have been removed. But, like any
abstraction not recognized as such, this can be misleading. It
may make one forget that it is only from their roots in this
actual flesh-and-blood intercourse that those formal systems draw such life as they have; for the whole idea of a
logical relation is only possible by virtue of the sort of agreement between men and their actions which is discussed by
Wittgenstein in the *Philosophical Investigations*. [*ISS*, pp.
125–126]

To conclude: in order to construct a logic (or theory
of any sort) one needs to have a notion of what following a rule involves; this notion is taught us by social
activity, where rule-following is a way of living before

it is or can be a theory about ways of living. But it cannot be taught to us by way of behavioristic imitation or associationism, for the ideas these methods themselves wish to implant "exist only in and through the ideas which are current in society" (*ISS,* p. 133). Hence, explanation in the social and historical sciences "is not the application of generalizations and theories to particular instances: it is like the tracing of internal relations" (ibid.). To a degree this is true even of the internal relations of physical systems, for the social existence of the scientist enters into his ability for, and therefore into his behavior towards, forming a *theory* about physical systems, but his social activity does not enter into the behavior of the systems themselves (cf. *ISS,* p. 128). But "meaningful" systems, into whose configuration the social behavior of men themselves enters, present a special challenge, one that Hume failed to see: ". . . that 'the idea we form of an object' does not just consist of elements drawn from our observation of that object in isolation, but includes the idea of connections between it and other objects" (*ISS,* p. 124).

The above long citation and comments indicate an element in Winch's thesis which exposes it to attack. The objection is that the thesis leads to relativism. The objection might be put this way: Explanatory theories, whether in the natural or social and historical sciences, derive "such life as they have" from the social activities of men. But this social life, filled as it is with "anomalies, imperfections and crudities," is notoriously variable. Knowledge, which derives from it, can only therefore be variable as well.

Winch's reply is that the objection supposes what it

needs to establish, if the objection is considered as
stemming from a more absolutistic thesis in science.
He readily admits that reality may be utterly different
from what any man thinks about it, but this does not
gainsay the fact that we can only think about it in terms
of the grammar we happen to be dealing with,
whether that of a natural or of a social science. Further,
the objection supposes that it enjoys some special sense
of what is the difference between real and unreal and
what is the concept of agreement with reality itself.
But these notions, as Winch has tried to argue, "themselves belong to our language" (*EA*, p. 12). Winch is
only applying, to a question raised especially by Collingwood and Max Weber, the implications of Wittgenstein's *Tractatus* view, as transformed in the *Philosophical Investigations,* that the "limits of language are
the limits of my world."

The above defense seems rather negative. A better
statement of Winch's answer, and a further
clarification of his thesis, can be found in the articles
collected in *EA*. There Winch tries to show that the
"grammars" of institutions—*one* of which is a concrete spoken language—are as much open to self-cor-
rection as they are to variability. The concept of integrity would be an example. Involving, as Winch thinks
it does, a commitment to shouldering responsibilities
in a person's society, its disappearance from the form
of life would be tantamount to the disappearance of a
society itself (cf. *EA.,* p. 70). Or again, Vico's triad of
birth, death, and sexual relations are "limiting concepts" of what we can possibly mean by the expression
'human life,' even though the particularities of this
triad differ widely from population to population (cf.

EA, pp. 43–47). And, of course, 'rationality' is one of the most striking "limiting concepts" of all. It is not induced, as Kant correctly saw (against Hume), but it is not a priori either (cf. *EA,* pp. 33, 179). These limiting concepts give us the criteria with which we do in fact operate in understanding. In a certain sense they give us the criteria of what we have to say, not because they are beyond all correction (as Kant thought) but because we would not know what it would be like to try to say something without them. But, within limits, they are self-correcting. The "grammar" of sex affects the "grammar" of birth; the "grammar" of economic behavior affects the "grammar" of political behavior; the "grammar" of rationality in the natural sciences affects the "grammar" of rationality in the social sciences (and vice versa). Winch contrasts his position with the extreme subjectivism of Sartre, for whom the initial possibility of a perspective is a matter of unlimited choice (cf. *EA,* p. 178). There is a dialectic in the evolution of life as well as in the evolution of language. He expresses this point clearly in considering what happens when a member of one culture tries to "understand" the culture of another:

> We have to create a new unity for the concept of intelligibility, having a certain relation to our old one and perhaps requiring a considerable realignment of our categories. We are not seeking a state in which things will appear to us just as they do to members of S [empathy model], and perhaps such a state is unattainable anyway. But we *are* seeking a way of looking at things which goes beyond our previous way [inductive model] in that it has in some way taken account of and incorporated the other way the members of S have of looking at things. Seriously to study another way

of life is necessarily to seek to extend our own—not simply to bring the other way within the already existing boundaries of our own, because the point about the latter in their present form, is that they *ex hypothesi* exclude that other. [*EA,* p. 33]

What is philosophy, then? It seems to be the game in which the corruption of "grammars" is especially exposed. But it is not a game that recommends some other, absolutistic grammar; and it, too, is a game that has its own limits and self-corrections. "[Philosophy] can no more show a man what he should attach importance to than geometry can show a man where he should stand" (*EA,* p. 191).

We may conclude this chapter with the following observations. Continental philosophers have often criticized analytic philosophy because of the rigid separation it makes between the worlds of fact and value, because it appears to propose a knowlege that leaves everything where it is, because it seems to avoid making judgments about what should be the case. Certainly, for hermeneutic philosophy on the Continent, from the time of Schleiermacher and Dilthey on, the attempt to overcome this fact/value dichotomy has become a primary touchstone of what it means to think hermeneutically. Whatever be the merits of this criticism of analytic philosophy generally, it cannot be made of the views of von Wright and Winch. Both of these authors attach the greatest importance to the role that action and freedom play in the development of understanding, though neither considers the range of freedom absolute. Von Wright observes but does not

pursue the connection between our ascription of responsibility and of intentionality to some event.
Winch clearly states that our concepts are derived from
the ongoing forms of life in our societies. Somehow
our aspirations, wants, desires, and interests are themselves hermeneutically, interpretatively, active in the
emergence of knowledge. Knowledge (or understanding) and interests (or purposes) are interwoven. The
following chapter offers another way of expressing
this fundamental hermeneutical insight.

2

A Psychosocial Hermeneutics

With this chapter we step across the channel and meet a rather different form of hermeneutical thought. Analytic philosophers, as mentioned earlier, are prone to constructing logical maps or "grammars" for a semantical process they find already in place. Continental philosophers, in contrast, are inclined to ask the genetic question, 'How did the process come to be that way?' 'What are the conditions for its occurring?' 'Do these conditions contain clues to the legitimacy of the subsequent process?' This is both a more Kantian and a more phenomenological kind of approach.

Why do Continental philosophers have this preference? One of the main reasons, I think, is an essentially moral one: an impression that a logicizing kind of philosophy tends to leave the social landscape just as it was. Sometimes it seems to have a vested interest in keeping the landscape as it was. It may appear to be a style of philosophizing which is inherently accommodating to the status quo, since it does not seem to propose a guide for rationally changing the status quo. Even when it is mapping the logical network of purposive action in a nonpositivist way—as is the case with von Wright and Winch—it makes no judgment of the worth of such purposiveness. It seems to be, in short, a philosophy that draws a map but cannot offer a critique—an impressive exercise, a Continental philosopher might say, for explaining the world but of little help for changing it.

For the sake of brevity I am admittedly oversimplifying the point here; but one can appreciate the substance of the charge. It has to do with the practical application of philosophy, of the relationship between theory and practice. One should also realize, however, that the analytic philosopher is in fact no less a humane and concerned citizen than his Continental counterpart, and no less interested in rational change. There are reasons for his approaching philosophy in the way he does. A mention of these at this stage may help the reader in three ways: it will help him appreciate some of the motivation underlying the approaches presented in the last chapter; it will help him understand why the Continental philosophers about to be considered think it necessary to concentrate on a practical approach; but it will also forewarn the reader of potential trouble spots and weaknesses in the Continental sorts of hermeneutics which we will present in this and the succeeding chapters.

For, needless to say, the phenomenologist assumes that the question about the constitution or genesis of a process is a legitimate question. But is it? No doubt everything hangs on the sense one will give to the word 'legitimate.' How this judgmental term may be acceptably explained from the side of two Continental philosophers will be the main burden of the next two chapters. For now, let us indicate briefly why current analytic philosophy has reservations about the possible success of such a project.

I think I have given already in Chapter One sufficient indication that von Wright and Winch certainly
do not enshrine a fact/value or theory/practice dichotomy in any simplistic sense of the term. It is clear that
for both of them intentionality plays a patent, indeed
essential, and in any case inescapable role in the constitution of any knowledge or understanding. Knowledge, understanding, motives, desires, interests, and
purposes are all interwoven—a thesis which will be
repeated in a different register in the chapters to come.
Nevertheless, this analytic friendliness toward the
Continentals has its limits.

Von Wright expresses the difference very clearly.
Speaking not so much of the differences between analytic and Continental philosophers but of the differences between "Galilean" and "Aristotelian" themes in
philosophizing, he remarks that, though each protects
some truthful insights, "there is also a basic opposition, removed from the possibility both of reconcilia-
tion and of refutation—even, in a sense, removed
from truth. It is built into the choice of primitives, of
basic concepts for the whole argumentation. This
choice, one could say, is 'existential.' It is a choice of a
point of view which cannot further be grounded"
(*EU*, p. 32). An aspect of this remark may be extended, I think, to the point I am making here.

Von Wright's mention of a basic choice that is "even,
in a sense, removed from truth" is an echo of Wittgenstein's thesis that every claim we make to or quest we
make for knowledge takes place itself within a system
that has its own set of presuppositions. Of these presuppositions one cannot use 'to know' in the same way
that one uses it elsewhere; nor do such presuppositions

have any other truth than their articulation into the foundations of our language-game. Nor is there any possible meta-justification of this system within some supersystem. According to Friedrich Waismann's notes, Wittgenstein once observed that one could take the rules according to which chess is played and make these the counters in a new game and that perhaps the rules of this new game would be the rules of logic. But then one would have simply a new game, on a par with the old, and "not a meta-game." Consequently, there is no theory of validation which one can offer for the justification of one set of rules over another: "the syntax cannot be justified" (cf. Wittgenstein 1967*b*, pp. 121–126).

It follows that the only legitimation one has in fact for the nest of presuppositions in which our thinking moves is our form of life itself, our *praxis*:

The *Vor Wissen* [set of presuppositions] is not propositional knowledge. . . . It is, one could say, a *praxis*. Giving grounds, however, justifying evidence, comes to an end;— but the end is not certain propositions striking us immediately as true, i.e., it is not a kind of seeing on our part; it is our acting, which lies at the bottom of the language-game. [von Wright 1972, p. 57]

For the happening-processes one finds in nature, von Wright remarks (in a reference to Kuhn's work on the history of science), there may possibly exist a unitary body of paradigms, trying to bring everything together, even if only momentarily. He holds that there does not seem to be, however, such a unitary body of paradigms for "action-processes," where meanings are developed and transmitted. Here, instead, there is ideological pluralism, which is itself the consequence of different interests (see von Wright 1972, p. 59).

In sum, von Wright—and Winch as well—are agreeing with the Continental philosophers that the worlds of knowing and action and evaluation are indeed interwoven; but they are saying, too, that there is no privileged standpoint outside this system from which to critique it securely.

The Continental philosophers agree that there is no presuppositionless, much less absolute or noncontingent, standard of critique that one may invoke here, but they do hold that there must be some method or some mechanism of evaluation that may come into play and be known if action and purposive change are to occur rationally.

Recall von Wright's phrasing, cited above: "basic opposition . . . in a sense removed from truth . . . choice of primitives . . . 'existential' . . . a choice of a point of view which cannot further be grounded." The kind of Continental hermeneutics which we will be reviewing in this and the succeeding chapter does not agree with this position, however sympathetic it may be in other aspects to von Wright's and Winch's theses. The task for the Continentals becomes one of finding a ground, something transcendental, perhaps even ontic, something antesemantical or antepredicative, which may be both an effective and a trustworthy guide for purposive discourse—that is, for a sound understanding in the areas of goals and motives. For Jürgen Habermas, in the present chapter, this ground will be an empirical thesis—stemming from Marxian and psychosociological studies—about socially evolving human nature. For Hans-Georg Gadamer, subject of the succeeding chapter, it will be an ontological thesis, stemming from Heidegger, about the linguistic nature of human existence.

We turn for the remainder of this chapter to the psychosocial hermeneutics of Jürgen Habermas.

Jürgen Habermas is the currently best-known heir of a twentieth-century movement in philosophy often referred to as the "Frankfurt School." This school has traditionally a strongly empiricist approach, characterized not so much by its aversion to all forms of German idealism—which other schools share—but by its election to seek stimulus and measure from studies in the social sciences. Habermas continues this tradition in his own way. His main works available in English which we shall use are *Knowledge and Human Interests* and *Theory and Practice* (hereafter referred to as *KI* and *TP*).

Habermas has always presented his thought in an exploratory and tentative way, often modifying the stress and sometimes the tenor of his views as discussion continued. One can find three phases in his writings, which we might term the negative, the positive, and the programmatic. In what follows we will touch on each of these.

The negative phase is characterized by a critique and rejection of a positivist brand of philosophy. This continues a shift already present in the Frankfurt School and in neo–Marxist thought generally. As one commentator puts it, "the critique of ontology, while still a requirement for critical theory, no longer has priority equal to that of a critique of science and technology as

ideology" (Misgeld 1976, p. 165). Thinkers close to
sociological studies are almost bound to be motivated
in this direction because of their sensitivity to the fact
that it is not just events that have significance but the
meanings that events take on in the eyes of members of
society. While causalist explanations may be appropriate for events, they do not work for the domain of
meanings. Hence some other concept of objectivity
must be sought for the domain of social interaction.

But, even more fundamentally (because more generally) than this, positivist philosophies of science fail
to realize that their approach either enshrines or recommends a certain ideal knowledge-situation for the
members of a society. It instantiates what it considers
to be the satisfaction of man's basic epistemological
aspirations. It contains, therefore, a philosophy of human nature. But it has no means of asking itself where
it got such a philosophy of man. It simply assumes
without argument that the ideal knowledge-situation
is a fulfillment of such epistemological interests as can
be assimilated to the ideals of the natural sciences.
These latter fulfill "technological" interests, as Habermas (in a somewhat wide sense of the term) calls them,
which are satisfied when we learn how to predict and
control the workings of natural processes. These are
causalist systems.

Is the rationality of these simply to be transposed to
the systems of personal relationships, which are the
domain of the social sciences? What would logically
result from this approach? For example, imagine that a
social problem were conceived, for all rational purposes, as simply a species of technical problem. In that
case, only experts could rationally discuss it and, even

in their own individual cases, only their expertise and not their personality or their humanity or their values would make a positive contribution to the discussion. What, after such a discussion, would be left for the mass of citizens who are not expert in this field? Only passive acceptance, submission, some thinly disguised program of indoctrination. In such a society, democracy, seen as an ideal of consensus achieved through the free discussion of all, would be finished. If, then, the brokers of power in a society, even if well intentioned, tried to identify and attempt satisfaction of intersubjective interests in terms modeled on the causalist and subjectless programs of the physical sciences, the result would be a society which would not increase but rather diminish the incidence of freedom in its citizenry. The moral here is not that the subjectless methodology of the physical sciences is inherently vicious but that it is the wrong basis for mapping the processes of intersubjective systems. As McCarthy, in his excellent study of Habermas, puts it, "The real problem . . . is not technical reason as such but its universalization, the forfeiture of a more comprehensive concept of reason in favor of the exclusive validity of scientific and technological thought, the reduction of *praxis* to *techne*, and the extension of purposive–rational action to all spheres of life" (McCarthy 1978, p. 22). Subjectless methodologies are appropriate for satisfying man's interests in confronting nature and mastering it—"instrumental interests," Habermas calls them. For "communicative interests," he holds, we would do better to consult the methodologies of the social sciences.

A key word in Habermas's thought has already sev-

eral times occurred here: 'interests.' Habermas means
by it the whole range of cognitive impulses, both for
theoretical and for practical goals, which is a part of
man's specific nature and not simply a form or preference that is accidentally derived from his culture—*human* interests, in short.

What is one looking for, when turning to the
methodologies of the social sciences? Suppose one
were to accept, without arguing it further, that people
in their intersubjective exchanges affect one another
rather by their "meanings"—the way a bouquet of
flowers affects the receiver—than by their physical or
causative impacts—the way the pollen on the blooms
might affect some allergic recipient. In this case one
needs a methodology for checking to see whether
meanings are being processed accurately. This is essential so that the participants in this exchange may
understand each other and hence plan and work in
concert. A methodology to this end will satisfy man's
"hermeneutical interests," where 'hermeneutical' in
this usage is taken in its restricted sense as a study
aiming at the accurate interpretation of texts.

But, continues Habermas, what if the disturbance in
the transmission of meanings comes not from the accidents of history or from the strangeness of the text, but
rather from the nature of the message—or even of the
medium—itself? What if the corruption is internal and
itself a distortion of man's interests toward intersubjectivity? In other words, what if man's interest in
communicating with his fellows is being thwarted because the very content of what is being communicated
is inimical to man's deeper interests in fellowship? In
this case, freedom to communicate becomes itself an

agency in the defeat of freedom. Habermas calls such a distortion or corruption not accidental or superficial, but "systematic" (cf. Habermas 1970*a*). For such a case we need something more than a mere methodology (like philology, for example) for the accurate detection of what the author meant. We need a methodology for reflecting on the worth of the meanings being transmitted. And since this methodology is itself a part, and a very critical (because evaluative) part, of the meanings the culture is transmitting, one needs a methodology that is inherently capable of assessing its own functioning—in short, capable of what Habermas calls "self-reflection."

This awkward term, which occurs frequently in *KI* and less often in later writings, may become clearer to us if we recall the sort of impact that some nationally traumatic event has upon a nation's consciousness—a mass suicide in Jonestown, for example. There is an enormous sadness on the occasion of an event like this, an immense regret over the senseless waste of life. But there is also, particularly among writers, educators, churchmen, and the like, a great deal of soul-searching about not merely the content but also the form of their functioning as interpreters and purveyors of their society's traditions. One asks not only about the *what* of educational processes but also about the *how* of an educating that gave few means of preventing (and perhaps even fostered) the surrender of freedom by so many to such a fanaticism. What Habermas would like to propose is a methodology that is capable of supporting this kind of self-investigation in the smooth as well as in the traumatic passages of a society's development—indeed, especially in the smooth, for it is characteristic of a successful distortion not to be noticed by those who are its victims. This quest Habermas sometimes phrases as an engagement in "depth hermeneutics."

In summary, then, on this question of interests one may say, following Habermas, that there are three levels on the road to freedom. One is the level of freedom from the resistance and capriciousness of nature, the human interest that science satisfies in supplying us with food, shelter, medicine, and the means of distribution. Another is the freedom to be in contact with one's past and with one's fellows, the interest satisfied by the typically interpretative or liberal arts, in giving us access to meanings and shared opinions that can form the basis for cooperative effort. The third is freedom from lingering internalized or institutionally externalized forms of distortion that promote or somehow ratify man's alienation from himself. This last is an interest man has in emancipation. It is a rather sophisticated need. It is not likely to be high in the consciousness of someone still struggling to get enough to eat. Failures in freedom at this level are correspondingly more subtle. The originality in Habermas's work is the way he tries to offer a strategy for the exposition and correction of such deeply buried distortions of freedom's ideals.

But of course, in order to distinguish between the corrupting internalizations or institutions and the progressive ones, he will need a philosophy of human nature that can guide him to the apprehension of man's truest and most profound tendencies. This cannot be found in the traditions of German idealism: positivism has definitively demythologized metaphysics. Further, it has "with remarkable subtlety and indisputable success" promoted a kind of epistemology which must contain elements of both the rationalist and empiricist traditions (*KI,* pp. 4–5). Habermas respects this much of positivism's ideal. What he needs, then, is a philosophy of human nature which is at once empirical and antimetaphysical and capable of keeping the interested individual in his role as both the one being studied and the one doing the studying. That is why Habermas finds his inspiration partly in Marxist traditions and partly in psychosocial studies. To show how Marx enters the equation is our first point in the exposition that follows. In a second point we will briefly mention Habermas's review of Kant, Hegel, Peirce, and Dilthey—philosophers whose thought is inadequate for Habermas's purposes but who nevertheless contribute positively in showing us routes which, though false, were tried for good reason. (It is the good reason that must be incorporated into a more satisfactory view.) These two points will demonstrate the positive phase of Habermas's thought. How psychoanalysis and psycholinguistics get into the picture will be our third point. How this may lead to freedom from alienation is our final point. These two elements illustrate the programmatic nature of his thought.

1. Kant and Hegel did take into account the interests of the human subject in the process of knowing. Kant saw him as a judge imposing order on the jumbled flow of sensations from a stabile position outside them. Hegel saw him as internally involved in a process of coming to know which was larger than himself and for whose evolution he was the chief though transitory medium. Both of these philoso-

phers saw the satisfaction of intellectual interests in the apprehension and application of symbolic systems, and both labeled reality in accord with these systems. In this sense both were idealists. Hegel was right, against Kant, in refusing to see the ego as a fixed subject. In his own identification of coming-to-know with coming-to-be, however, Hegel made man's fulfillment-in-being the effect of his fulfillment-in-knowing.

It is, Marx answered, rather the opposite: it is man's interests-in-being that determine his interests in knowing, which make him a "knower."

What are these interests-in-being? Marx answers that the very conditions of human existence show them to us: "[Man] confronts the substance of nature itself as a natural power. He sets in motion the natural forces belonging to his corporeal being, that is, his arms and legs, head, and hand, in order to appropriate nature in a form usable for his own life" (cited in *KI,* pp. 27–28). The name for this appropriation is *labor.* It is a species-interest, "independent of all forms of society, a perpetual necessity in nature in order to mediate the material exchange between man and nature, in other words, human life" (cited in *KI,* p. 27). This interest, in so far, is like that of any animal, human or not. But men began "to distinguish themselves from animals as soon as they began to produce their means of subsistence" (cited in *KI,* p. 41). It was in the interests of this production, and not in that of an idealist construction of symbolic systems, that men employed their reason. "That is why," writes Habermas, "labor, or work, is not only a fundamental category of human existence but also an epistemological category" (*KI,*

p. 28). In this perspective a satisfactory knowing is equivalent to a satisfactory knowing-how-to-appropriate. In employing their reasoning powers on problems in the satisfaction of their needs, men created a history. The history of productive labor, then, as the account of man's appropriation of natural forces for the satisfaction of his needs, is the natural history of man.

Habermas agrees with this assessment in part. Marx correctly identified one species-bound interest. It is the instrumentalist cognitive interest that the natural sciences are understood as seeking to satisfy. But Marx, because of his materialist presuppositions, went on to reduce all intellectual interests to the empirical methods of this instrumentalist category. In consequence he made it impossible for himself to answer a problem which he better than any other described-the problem of class divisions.

It is true that man produces himself, shapes the evolution of his species, in his manner of work. To that degree it is true that labor is self-reflexive. But nature is not immediately given to man as it is to other animals. "Nor," adds Marx, "is the human mind *(Sinn)* in its immediate, subjective form the same as human sensuousness" (cited in *KI,* p. 28). Man exercises a creative, transforming work on nature; he is in a special way independent of nature. This is his subjectivity, in contrast to the objectivity of nature. Labor is the externalized synthesizing of these subjective and objective factors. Man's independence is not to be understood in an idealist sense, however. The forms of labor "are categories not primarily of the understanding but of objective activity; and the unity of the objectivity of

possible objects of experience is formed not in transcendental consciousness but in the behavioral system
of instrumental action" (*KI,* p. 34). Our knowledge-
interests, therefore, are confined to "our interest in
possible technical control over natural processes" (*KI,*
p. 35). Anything else is illusory.

The subjectivity of man, however, cannot be fully
clarified in this analysis. The objectivity of nature does
not appear at all the same to men of different genera-
tions: "each generation, on the one hand, continues its
acquired activity under entirely altered circumstances
and, on the other, modifies the old circumstances with
an entirely altered activity" (cited in *KI,* p. 325 n. 37).
The reasons for this change are primarily changes in
the methods of labor. Instrumental action is the unity
that binds all consciousnesses together to make one
human continuity. But can instrumental action alone
bear the burden of unifying consciousnesses? Marx
thought that it could, and in so thinking left the way
open to a positivist reduction of cognitive interests to
instrumentalist interests. There are clear hints in
Marx, Habermas claims, that something more is
required, but Marx's reduction of the self-generative
act of the species to the conditions of labor prevents
his resolving the antimony that he described (cf. *KI,*
p. 42).

The antinomy consists in this. Marx saw that
configurations of consciousness—'ideologies'—are obstacles to human progress; but these are systems of
symbolic interaction and exchange. Having rejected
Kantian and Hegelian epistemologies, which sought
to explain the synthesis of consciousness at the symbolic level, Marx tried to achieve a foundation for the

synthesis of consciousnesses at the technological level. It is a kind of category mistake, an effort to apply to symbolic interactions a set of analyses which not only do not explain them but actually presuppose them. For labor, of course, is a social activity. But what Marx finds wrong, for example, in a capitalist system of labor is not that the workers cooperate, but that they cooperate as mere combinations, not "of their own accord" but as mere animated links of machinery themselves (*KI,* pp. 51–52). Capitalism, in short, is a fault in class consciousness and not in the rationality of technological action. Technological procedures might very well—indeed probably would—remain the same whether the workers were combined "of their own accord" or not. In this sense it is not purely a form of technology that defines capitalism. The natural restraints on man's development, which technological action is designed to overcome, remain basically the same, whether in the past or in the present, whether in a capitalist or in a noncapitalist society. Ideological restraints on man's development, however, are internal ones. It is upon these that exploitative systems of technological action rest. These internalized symbolic systems, then, are what engender man's alienation, his loss of self-awareness and of self-achievement.

Are, as Marx thought, these internalized codes purely the result of materialist productive systems? No, Habermas argues. They are more accurately the result of certain forms of social consciousness which the power centers of the society define, sustain, and transmit. The proof of this is the fact that identical instrumentalities of production and distribution co-exist with very different forms of social conscious-

ness—for example, in the oil-producing industries.
The conclusion is that ideologies are not automatically
caused by or matched with methods of production;
neither are they in-born. They must be taught. It is,
needless to say, a "subject" who teaches them. And
this subject, in teaching, is fulfilling his or someone's
interests.

Habermas concludes, then, that Marx succeeded in
identifying an area of cognition that is both empirical
and self-reflexive, where cognition and interests are
interwoven. He did not succeed in showing them to be
the same thing. What is needed, to complement (and
correct) Marx's critique of consciousness externalized
in labor, is a critique of social attitudes internalized in
the consciousness of subjects.

2. Where shall we look for the beginnings of such a
critique? Not, as mentioned earlier, in the classics of
German metaphysics, but rather in the classics of the
philosophy of science, though not in the positivist
ones—hence the attention Habermas gives to the philosophies of Charles Sanders Peirce and of Wilhelm
Dilthey.

Peirce for the natural sciences and Dilthey for the
cultural ones move in the direction of formulating the
method of critique needed, but neither finally suc-
ceeds.

Old-style and modern positivism had defined truths
in terms of a correspondence theory between symbol
and reality, where the individual subject disappears as
a determining point of reference (cf. *KI*, pp. 67–69).
Peirce, in contrast, defined truth in terms of subjectivity or, more accurately, in terms of intersubjectivity,
since an emerging consensus among the community

of investigators is needed to cancel out what remains in an opinion of the accidental and arbitrary:

All human thought and opinion contains an arbitrary, accidental element, dependent on the limitations in circumstances, power, and bent of the individual; an element of error, in short. But human opinion universally tends in the long run to a definite form, which is the truth. Let any human being have enough information and exert enough thought upon any question, and the result will be that he will arrive at a certain definite conclusion, which is the same that any other mind will reach under sufficiently favorable circumstances. [*KI,* p. 93]

Where positivism defines the possibilities of knowledge in the analysis of a presumed instance of knowledge already constituted and taken as normative, Peirce analyzes the constitution of this knowledge in the first place and, thereby, the conditions actually experienced in bringing this knowledge about: "it is necessary to consider science as living, and therefore not as knowledge already acquired but as the concrete life of men who are working to find out the truth" (cited in *KI,* p. 94). In this way, Habermas believes, Peirce restores *praxis,* to recall Wittgenstein's term, and the subject as an essential reference point.

Intersubjectivity as a fundamental condition for the possibility of knowledge then leads Peirce to the role that language plays and to the semiotic dimension:

Man makes the word, and the word means nothing which the man has not made it to mean, and that only to some man. But . . . man can think only by means of words or other eternal symbols. . . . In fact, therefore, men and words reciprocally educate each other; each increase of a man's information involves, and is involved by, a corresponding increase of a word's information. [*KI,* p. 332]

In passing, one may note the degree to which this view of Peirce foreshadows that of Peter Winch. Habermas, like Winch, also stresses the connection between sociology and epistemology, as we must show further on. Peirce, however, after introducing this semiotic and intersubjective dimension, goes on to elaborate it in a way which is acceptable neither to Winch nor to Habermas.

When Peirce analyzes the nature of this semiotic dimension he defines it in terms of instrumentalist (pragmatistic) behavior: "In order to ascertain the meaning of an intellectual conception one should consider what practical consequences might conceivably result by necessity from the truth of that conception; and the sum of the consequences will constitute the entire meaning of that conception" (cited in *KI,* 335).

Even Peirce, however, recognizes that such terms as 'consider,' 'consequences,' 'by necessity' in the above passage indicate that the semiotic dimension is not simply resolvable in the flow of action; it precedes the action, as defining its possibilities, and remains after it: "[Statements refer to] the 'would–acts,' 'would–do's' of habitual behavior; and no agglomeration of actual happenings can ever completely fill up the meaning of a 'would-be'" (cited in *KI,* p. 121). This semiotic dimension, then, which is as essential to Peirce's intersubjectivity as his intersubjectivity is to knowledge, is not reducible to instrumentalist behavior. It remains as a transcendental condition for the existence of a community of investigators, but one which Peirce's analysis does not succeed in clarifying. However astutely Peirce analyzes the relation of language to objective nature, or even the relation of the solitary mind working in the laboratory to nature, he fails to explain (though his theory supposes it) the relations of minds to each other. Habermas concludes:

> . . . the communication of investigators requires the use of language that is not confined to the limits of technical control over objectified natural processes. It arises from symbolic interaction between societal subjects who reciprocally know and recognize each other as unmistakable individuals. This *communicative action* is a system of reference that cannot be reduced to the framework of *instrumental action*. [*KI,* p. 137]

It is, nevertheless, the great merit of Peirce to have identified, from within the logic of science, this intellectual interest in communicative action and to have shown how it underlies even the technological interests of science. It marks an advance over the naturalism of Marx, while it retains a basic aspect of Marx's position: namely, that self-development in the pursuit of truth is primarily a community enterprise, the development of a species–specific interest rather than of an individual one.

Working from an entirely different perspective, Dilthey also sought an understanding of our species-interest in communicative action. Since Dilthey's position has been discussed in the introduction, it will suffice here to give Habermas's account of his theory.

Dilthey, we remember, held that experience does

not give us nature in an immediately intelligible form. That is why the natural sciences must construct mathematical models, which, by their explanatory power, mediate the subject's understanding of natural processes. Experience of a cultural object, however, is immediately intelligible, not perhaps always in its phenomenal details, but at least in its being the epiphany of a life-world in which we all share. At this level of transaction, no mediating agency of understanding is required, nor could any be constructed. This is the basis for distinguishing the protocol experience of the cultural sciences from that of the natural sciences. It is summed up in Dilthey's adaptation of Vico, "he who *studies* history is the same as he who *makes* history." But this triggers the ancient Socratic dilemma: If one makes history, must he not know what it is he is making—and then what need is there to study it? Or, if one needs to study history, must he not stand apart from it and construct a model to mediate his understanding of it—and, if he does, what remains of the difference between the natural sciences and the cultural sciences? Dilthey recognized the dilemma: "Interpretation would be impossible if the expressions of life were totally alien. It would be unnecessary if there were nothing alien in them. [Hermeneutics] thus lies between these two extreme opposites. It is required wherever there is something alien that the art of understanding has to assimilate" (cited in *KI,* p. 164). But this suggests that hermeneutics is not a universal problem after all. It would shrink, in practice, to the sometime usefulness of a methodology, with the usual Cartesian goals of validity and certainty (cf. *KI,* p. 182).

In Habermas's view, Dilthey's turning in this way to

methodology is not of itself fatal. It is not methodology as such that is ruinous for self-reflection in the
version Habermas requires, but rather a particular
kind of methodology—one, namely, that displaces the
subject from a position internal to the experience. This
is the way of positivism. Habermas contends that
Dilthey, in spite of himself, succumbed to its tempta-
tion. This is shown, for example, in his election of
philology as the model science:

> The first condition [writes Dilthey] of the construction of
> the historical world is thus the regeneration of mankind's
> confused and in many ways corrupted memories of itself
> through critique correlated with interpretation. Therefore
> the basic historical science is philology in the formal sense of
> the scientific study of languages, in which tradition has been
> sedimented; the collection of the heritage of earlier men; the
> elimination of errors contained therein; and the chronologi-
> cal order and combination that put these documents in in-
> ternal relation with each other. In this philology is not the
> historian's aid but the basis of his procedure. [*KI*, p. 216]

It might not have been so. Had Dilthey been in a
position to interpret the hermeneutic circle in a different way he might have found the solution he was seeking to the dilemma. If, for example, he could have seen
the hermeneutic circle in dialectical fashion wherein
the interpreter, instead of having to move outside the
circle to the Kantian position of judge, stayed within it
and, in Hegelian fashion, realized that the movement
of the general is accomplished only within the dialogue of particulars, then he would not have destroyed
the concrete life-context from which understanding

can only emerge phenomenologically and which it cannot transcend. Habermas writes:

Hermeneutics must assimilate the dialectic of the general and the individual that determines the relation of objectivation and experience and comes to expression *as such* in the medium of the "common." If this is so, then understanding itself is bound to a situation in which at least two subjects communicate in a language that allows them to share—that is, to make communicable through intersubjectively valid symbols—what is absolutely unsharable and individual. Hermeneutic understanding ties the interpreter to the role of a partner in dialogue. Only this *model of participation in communication learned in interaction can explain the specific achievements of hermeneutics.* [*KI,* pp. 179–180]

Dilthey was right in noting the self-reflexivity inherent in the cultural sciences and in seeing that the interests of communicative action are peculiarly interwoven in their object. The special nature, however, of this communicative action was lost, became inaccessible to elucidation, in Dilthey's moving the "understander" back to the subjectless role of the scientific observer. What is needed is some way other than that of the philologist in which to solve the problem of how language, though a general and theory-impregnated system, is also individual and practical (cf. *KI,* pp. 171–172). This is a problem that the formalist and pragmatist theories of the sciences and Dilthey's theory of history fail to solve; but, wrote Habermas in 1968, "psychoanalysis, if we comprehend it as a general theory of life-historical self-formative processes, provides an answer to it" (*KI,* p. 186).

3. The appearance at this point of psychoanalysis as a candidate for a rational model, and indeed for the fundamental rational model, may strike some as surprising, even shocking—a desperate grasping at straws. It is not a turn likely to endear Habermas to orthodox Marxists, ensconced, as von Wright drily observes of them, in their "windowless chambers" (*EU,* p. 160). But it is important to an understanding of Habermas's position to see that psychoanalysis, or something like it, is the positive implicate of his critique of Marx, Peirce, and Dilthey. If it didn't exist, its analogue would have to be invented. The following remarks, though slightly repetitious, may make the choice seem less arbitrary.

Marx, as we have said, identified labor as the species-interest where man both defines and furthers his nature as man. The rationalization of labor-processes is tantamount to human progress. But Marx rested everything on the rationalizations that science could offer for these processes.

Science, however—especially the mechanistic science with which Marx was familiar—rationalized action on nature in terms of a formal language. This formal language is by definition subjectless and does not incorporate the contingent point of view of the researcher in its formulas. Three features characterize the instrumentalist use of this language when it is applied to the world: (i) it synthesizes or unifies experience in terms of measurement; the function of the subject is to read these measurements in terms of a calculus which makes sense of them; (ii) communication between experimenters is restricted to information about a purposive–rational utilization of means; and (iii) "individual experience is eliminated in favor of repeatable results of instrumental action" (*KI*, p. 193). If this rationalization, designed for instrumentality, is nevertheless applied to the behavior of men, then it can only be that human relations are bound to move in the direction of instrumentalist patterns, with the result that dialogue is destroyed and men treat each other as objects. This is precisely what Marx did not want, but it is a result to which the logic of his instrumentalization of cognitive interests was bound to lead.

Peirce, too, though starting from a different place, lapsed into a formalist account of the language in which the community of investigators could communicate. The same, *mutatis mutandis,* is to be said of Dilthey, in his election of philology.

What is needed is an account of language that satisfies its usage as an ongoing system of mutual understanding, for this is, after all, supposed even by its instrumental usages in the natural sciences. Such an account must meet the following two demands: (i) it must respect the fact that in dialogic usage—the level at which we converse with one another—language usage and language interpretation occur on the same plane, immanently, without the need to retreat to a hierarchical meta-language (cf. *KI,* p. 172); and (ii) it must offer a methodical explanation of this fact, one whose logical articulation is clear and accessible for empirical confirmation (cf. *KI,* p. 173). In such a language, the instrumentalist equation (subject–object) would be replaced by the dialogic one (subject–partner) (cf. *KI,* p. 181). However, the objectivity potentially available in the latter equation can be threatened by distortions of symbolic structures which may come from either the subject or the partner. The model required, then, must offer from within its own resources a way of revealing and overcoming such possible distortions. This is why, Habermas initially held, the psychoanalytic model, rethought as a hermeneutic of dialogue, is "relevant to us as the only tangible example of a science incorporating methodical self-reflection" (*KI,* p. 214).

Dilthey, as was mentioned, looked to philology as the model science for overcoming cultural distortions and for obtaining objectively valid comprehension. But philology, Habermas argues, cannot attain the hermeneutical depth that is required. It is the object of philology to reveal the original intention of the text beneath the corruptions laid upon it by time and accident. Philology is successful when it recovers the conscious intention of the author, overcoming the external and accidental obstacles to the understanding of the text and hence bringing about the restoration of communication. One understands the text by removing the obstacles. But there are deeper corruptions which are internal to the text itself. To understand this sort of corruption is the aim of psychoanalysis: "the symbolic structures that psychoanalysis seeks to comprehend are corrupted by the impact of *internal* conditions. The mutilations have meaning *as such*" (*KI,* p. 217). Psychoanalysis is successful when it reveals how the corruption itself has a meaning, even if an unconscious one. In philology it is a problem of time's estranging the author; in psychoanalysis, of the author's estranging himself.

This accounts for the significance of dreams. The author himself does not understand them. A hermeneutics modeled on philology as an attempt to recover the intention of the author could not decipher them. Of dreams, Freud writes, "There must be one force here which is seeking to express something and another which is striving to prevent its expression" (cited in *KI*, p. 222). Both are partially successful. The impulsive forces do bring to expression what they want to say, but the inhibiting forces succeed in checking intelligibility by shifting the expression into a semantic form in which the original intention is unrecognizable. This is repression meted out by the subject himself. It takes the form of short-circuiting continuity between desire and its semantic expression (between interest and knowing): *"the speaking and acting subject's communication with himself is interrupted"* (*KI*, p. 217). In attempting, therefore, to restore continuity between desire and expression, psychoanalysis wishes to accomplish something that is at once experiential and semiotic, affective and cognitive, a matter both of interest and of knowledge: *"the act of understanding* to which [psychoanalysis] leads is self-reflection" (*KI*, p. 228). If this effort can be successful, the Marxian ideal of self-appropriation can be fulfilled at the semiotic or symbolic level. In suggesting a way for unblocking the flow of self-development, psychoanalysis provides a method for "a general interpretation of self-formative processes" (*KI*, p. 254).

But there is an un-Marxian supposition here which must be made explicit. Where in Marx the obstacles to self-formation are the institutionalized patterns of production and distribution, in psychoanalysis the obstacles are deformations institutionalized in language: "The ego's flight from itself is *an operation that is carried out in and with language*. Otherwise it would not be *possible to reverse the defensive process hermeneutically, via the analysis of language*" (*KI,* p. 241).

Freud saw this, but he lost the therapeutic practicality of this insight when, child of his times, he too adopted a mechanistic theory of explanation. Working out his theory, Freud reverted to the physicist's model of instincts as energy impulses being countered and transformed by other energy bundles within society. Freud's philosophy of history, then, simply replaced Marx's transcendental mechanism of labor with a transcendental mechanism of biological instincts. But, writes Habermas:

> The conception of the instincts as the prime mover of history and of civilization as the result of their struggle forgets that we have only *derived* the concept of impulse privatively from language deformation and behavioral pathology. At the human level we never encounter any needs that are not already interpreted linguistically and symbolically affixed to potential actions. [*KI,* p. 285]

In other words Habermas, like Winch, is stressing the point that language is not simply an interesting cultural deposit but is also an epistemological pool, which in shaping our forms also shapes the content of our knowledge and hence our ideal of truth.

Because Freud's physicalist base was too narrow a model for elucidating the human self-formative process, Habermas says we must refer to the practice of Freud rather than to his theory: "*The language of the theory is narrower than the language in which the technique was described*" (*KI,* p. 245). If we consult the passages where Freud discusses his practice, we find him well aware that the restoration of an interrupted self-formative process is not achieved purely at the semiotic and conceptual level, even though it is achieved through the use of language. Merely filling the gaps in a person's information about himself would, says Freud, "have as much influence upon the symptoms of nervous illness as a distribution of menu-cards in a time of famine has upon hunger" (cited in *KI,* p. 230). The illness is not an ignorance but a resistance and a repression at the affective level. In the psychoanalytic cure, then, the separation of the subject domain, thought of in the Kantian manner as a pure logical subject, from the object domain, thought of neutrally as the empirical sciences think of their objects, would be overcome: the subject would be restored to an integration of intelligence, desire, and performance.

In his 1968 *Knowledge and Human Interests,* Habermas developed in some detail a logic of self-reflection modeled on psychoanalysis. He has now, however, abandoned this approach in favor of another, modeled on language theory: the doctor—patient equation of the earlier investigation is replaced by the sender—receiver equation of modern linguistics. This shift is, in reality, a logical move for Habermas to make, and it is more promising intellectually.

It is more logical because language is more immediately a social phenomenon than is the psychic condition of an individual. As the main phenomenon for investigation it fits better, therefore, with Habermas's Marxian anthropology, where man's nature is defined socially before it is defined individually. It also fits better with Habermas's rational aims, because he holds the view (stemming from Peirce) that we should think of objectivity as the quality of a set of opinions that can be successfully argued rather than as a quality of the perception of things. The primordial importance of discourse, therefore, though already present in psychoanalysis, is heightened in turning to linguistics as a model for a self-reflecting logic of inquiry. Finally, Habermas's need for a notion of soundness, against which to contrast distortions in the free converse of all with all, may be more satisfactorily met in a linguistic approach than in a psychoanalytic one. It remains true, however, that because Habermas always focused on the dialogic features of Freud's theory, the transition from one model to the other is quite consistent with his long-term aims.

Habermas admits that his ideas in this later investigation are tentative and programmatic. He calls his work an effort in "universal pragmatics," and what he seeks to uncover are certain "dialogue-constitutive universals" that would be a form of species-competence for communication lying even deeper than Chomskyan language-competence (see Habermas, 1970*b* , pp. 367–373). For example, Habermas will point out that the fact of language itself—even if distorted in performance—is already a witness to man's species-need for a communication with his fellow man in an atmosphere free of mistrust and domination. Along this tack, Habermas will try to show the way in which the norms of justice, freedom, and truth are conceptually interwoven at this deeper level and will demonstrate that to violate one is to violate the others. In this way, he will try to show that theory and practice can be vindicated as indivisible.

These last remarks about the linking of truth, justice, and freedom lead us to our final point, Habermas's view of man's interest in emancipation.

4. This major point in Habermas's theory is at once the feature with which we can feel most easily sympathetic and the one most difficult to characterize satisfactorily. We are dealing now with semiotic distortions, blockages, corruptions. We mean distortions that exist semiotically, not merely those that are manifested semiotically. To show the difference, let us use as illustration of the latter some typical magazine advertisement for cigarettes: we see young, handsome, healthy people rejoicing as they light up. To illustrate the former let us think of a notion of deep prejudice—the idea, say, that to be black or white or brown or Catholic or Jew or Muslim is, in a Sartrean phrase, to be afflicted with a "metaphysical taint" (metaphysical because no empirical evidence is allowed to falsify it). The sway of these two distortions is different. Nature itself will serve as a check and test of the semiotic transmission 'smoking fits fine with fun and health.' But nature does not check out the worth of a prejudicial transmission; it is not straightforwardly falsifiable. Habermas stresses this all-important structural difference in semiotic transactions. It is a difference that calls for a different logic of exposition and evaluation.

What makes it difficult for us to uncover the need and nature of such a logic, Habermas continues, is the fact that these semiotically existing transmissions have become, in a way, nature or pseudonature or "second nature," "because the interactions occur in a setting which is not freely accessible to the consciousness of the actors: they are acting [as recipients of their social "grammar"] under the violence of intentions which are not immediately their own" (Habermas 1974, p. 48). Habermas's task, then, is to propose a set of ideal speech conditions where discourse may be seen to reveal both the possibility of and the criteria for unmasking discourse's own corruptions.

This is a little like hoping to raise oneself by one's own bootstraps, and it will be relevant to recall the earlier Wittgensteinian remarks as interpreted by von Wright, who concludes that the final solution here must be an ideology—that is, a group-belief clustered around a common interest, not itself subject to logical dissolution. But Habermas clearly hopes to have more than that.

His task when using the earlier psychoanalytic model was easier, for there the transaction was one to one, between doctor and patient, and aimed at the therapeutic goal that the patient become integrated with his own deepest (i.e., 'species') aspirations. In that model the neuroses of the society were simply the neuroses of the individual writ large: "The same configurations that drive the individual to neurosis move society to establish institutions" (*KI,* p. 276). The therapeutic moment was also characterized in psychoanalytic terms as a kind of illumination or moment of self-awareness, which the individual would first experience as a self-freeing and then presumably convey to the outside as a social emancipation.

How this emancipatory moment may occur in terms of the later linguistic model it is not easy to say. Habermas explores suggestions arising in the developmental psychology of such researchers as Jean Piaget and Lawrence Kohlberg. What is characteristic of these theses is their structuralist nature—that is, the hypothesis that the species itself contains *in potentia* levels of cognitive and moral development which various environments will activate with greater or lesser efficiency and success. This fits well with the type of "philosophy of history with practical intent" that Habermas is trying to develop (cf. Habermas 1973, pp. 201 ff), and, correlatively, it militates against the so-called social learning and positivist kind of psychological theory, which denies a native developmental structure and holds that all grammars are simply received *ab externo*.

Following Marx we have discovered one level of human interest which, because it is directed to the prediction and control of nonhuman forces, we call the technological interest. The natural sciences are especially concerned with this interest.

With Peirce and Dilthey we have identified another level of human interest which, because it is directed to cooperative relations with our fellows, we call the communicative interest. The historical, philological, and anthropological sciences are especially concerned with this interest.

Finally, with Freud, we have uncovered a level of human interest in which man wants to identify his cognitive patterns generally and test them for distortions and no-longer-justified controls. This we call man's emancipatory interest. Philosophy as anchored in the psychosocio–linguistic sciences is especially concerned with this interest.

These areas of interest set the conceptual boundaries, the critera, for the way the phrase 'rational society' can be intelligently used. The three together —appropriation by work, communication, and the practice of critique—characterize any given society. As is clear, the emancipatory interest, with its method of critical hermeneutics, is the main task, because it alone has the capacity to include the other two in its researches. The natural sciences methodologically exclude the subjective level of interest from their work, and they are right to do so (cf. *KI,* p. 315). The historico-philological sciences aim at the elucidation of a past or foreign interest. They, too, are right to discount the interests of the researcher himself (cf. *KI,* p. 316). Only a philosophy anchored in the social sciences can have a methodology that can contain and reflect back the interests of the researcher himself. Only this approach would, in short, have the power of self-reflection. Since, as Marx showed, there is no such thing as interest-free ("value-free") knowledge, the critical need now is to find a method of knowledge whereby the governing interests can be exposed, held to account, and corrected in the interests of truth, justice, and freedom.

3

Ontological Hermeneutics

The first German edition of Hans-Georg Gadamer's *Wahrheit und Methode (Truth and Method)* appeared in 1960. By then the phenomenological movement was turning toward language as the key manifestation of the way in which a person constructs his world. The shift toward language was abetted from an entirely different quarter as the model of structural linguistics began to be applied to theories of anthropology and literature (cf. Pettit 1975). The original thesis of phenomenology, that meaning occurs as a given prior to any conscious action, came to suggest that language occurs in some sense before speech. Gadamer, following Heidegger, sought to explain this insight through our experience of language. In *Truth and Method* he retained the Diltheyan word *hermeneutics,* but in the transformed sense given it by Heidegger, for describing the new philosophical task. His book had an immediate impact. More than any other, Gadamer made hermeneutics the identifying label for a new form of philosophy.

In an epilogue to the third edition of *Truth and Method,* Gadamer says that he chose his title—the separation by 'and' connoting a certain "tension" *(Spannung)*—in a deliberately polemical spirit. He wished to challenge in a constructive way the steady march of empiricist methods into the field of the human sciences. In the discussion following the first edition, various spokesmen, needless to say, rose to the challenge.

Among those willing to adopt some sort of hermeneutical perspective on the human sciences, two philosophical orientations developed. They came to be distinguished by the labels "critical" and "ontological." Habermas is a leading exponent of the former, Gadamer of the latter. Applying 'critical' to Habermas's work is not, of course, intended to suggest that Gadamer's analyses are somehow slack. 'Critical' was chosen in this context to indicate a nearer affinity to the Kantian project of stating the conditions for reliability in knowledge, with its inclination to look for models in the empirical and comparative sciences, and also for its contention that given meanings are not trustworthy as they stand. There is a somewhat aggressive note in "critical" hermeneutics. Habermas, for example, concludes his 1965 inaugural address at Frankfurt with the remark that the search for truth in our time can be pursued "only on the ruins of ontology" (*KI,* p. 317).

The dispute, nevertheless, has many of the earmarks of a family quarrel: the opponents share as much as they contest. This holds particularly for their agreement on an epistemological point, that the Kantian split between subject and object is untenable and that some sort of dialectical epistemology is essential; they also agree on a moral point, that knowledge which does not move by intrinsic impulse to application is in some degree deficient.

Despite its title Gadamer's work, as he has fre-

quently protested, is not anti-methodological. He
does argue that the pretension of any methodology
(positivist or not) to see itself as epistemology—that is,
to collapse the conditions of truth into those of the
right application of a technique—is "blind" (Gadamer
[German edition], 1975, "Nachwort," p. 518); and he
has Habermas in mind in that judgment. Gadamer sees
his own work as an attempt to fulfill the deepest aspirations of all methodologies. He wishes to make clear,
beneath method, the fundamental conditions for
truth's coming to light not simply as the result of a
technique—of something that the *subject* does—but as
a result of something that "happens to us over and
above our wanting and doing" (Gadamer [English
edition], 1975*a,* p. xvi; hereafter, *TM*). Only in this
way, he thinks, can the Kantian ghost of the knower as
judge be definitely exorcised. It follows that his own
method cannot employ deductive or inductive techniques. It must be phenomenological—that is, a descriptive method that will highlight and refine constants in experience (cf. *TM,* pp. xiv–xv).

Truth and Method is a far-ranging and difficult work.
One can scarcely expect to do justice to it in the scope
of this chapter. The "experience," for example, referred to in the above paragraph includes the exercises
of philosophical reflection carried out in the works of
many of the great philosophers of the West, from Plato
to Heidegger. Gadamer devotes considerable space to
them and argues an interpretation that is frequently
original, though not arbitrary or eccentric. But there is
another reason that makes Gadamer's work difficult
for the reader of philosophy in English-language traditions. It will be helpful to begin with a consideration of

this. The title of Gadamer's book indicates its importance. It is his conception of truth.

Gadamer's Conception of Truth

It is almost axiomatic for philosophical readers on this side of the Atlantic to think of truth as an attribute of sentences, not of things. It is a point on which the later Wittgenstein agreed with the earlier. This seems reasonable. If someone says it is true that his nephew had scrambled eggs for breakfast that morning, the avowal of truth does not add another detail to the human, culinary, or temporal characteristics of the event reported but only registers the speaker's belief that the linguistic description offered of the event is accurate as it stands. In other words, the addition of 'true' or 'false' to a sentence adds nothing to the description the sentence offers of external reality.

In such a view, either 'true' or 'false' comes into play only at the end of a process that begins with experiencing, passes by way of a conceptual ordering of impressions, and issues in an enunciation. It is only to the enunciation that these predicates apply.

Gadamer does not take issue with the soundness of this semantic version of truth when it is confined to its own sphere. But he argues that this must rest upon the soundness of another version of truth—an ontological version. In Gadamer's terminology, the semantic version consecrates a split between consciousness and the assertion that is the result of its act. But what about the experience that is the original impetus toward this assertion? Cannot 'true' be somehow said of that? If not, then it seems impossible to avoid saying that consciousness inserts itself, in either a Kantian or a nominalistic way, between experience and truth; and in that case, what could be left of the objectivity the sciences aim for?

To put it another way, if 'truth' is applied only to sentences, then it comes into play only as a side-effect of something that we do. For example, we do perceive something and we say 'That's an apple tree.' That may be called 'intuitive' truth. But in scientific contexts, the sentences to which 'true' can apply are the result of arguments and experiments—even more narrowly something that we "do." This is what Gadamer wants to challenge in its exclusivity: there is a truth, he holds, that happens "over and above our wanting and doing." We always go on the assumption, 'We find the truth'; Gadamer wants to bring out another aspect: 'Truth finds us.'

Somehow or other, Gadamer holds, we must rethink the medieval thesis of the convertibility of truth and being—that where one applies, the other applies as well. The burden of his book is to show that it is not just truth and expression but truth and reality that are interwoven, and this before expression occurs. The way in which truth can inhere in a "givenness that is not itself the object of intentional acts" (*TM,* p. 216) must become clear. In Gadamer's view, truth appears with its own authority in consciousness, and consciousness is, to a degree, passive in this reception. How can this notion be clarified? Heidegger, Gadamer thinks, points our analyses in the right direction.

In *Being and Time* (Heidegger 1962, pp. 312 ff.), Heidegger argues that human existing *(Dasein)* occurs as a givenness of meanings before an active intention reflects on them. Human existence itself is already a projection of a world of structures that constitute its possibilities in life. Some of these are neglected, some ratified and pursued. In either case, this neglect or ratification of "fore-meanings" constitutes the "self-disclosure" of human existence. The nature of self, then, appears within an ongoing projection of meanings and is not imposed on existence from an ideal, atemporal point outside the flow. In this sense, existence precedes essence, meanings precede deliberate consciousness of them, the possibilities of truth precede their capturing in sentences.

But these meanings, appearing in human existence, are structures with a past and a future. The essence of human existence, then, which is their disclosure, is temporality. Inasmuch as human existence is the only place in which being appears, being itself is time. Thus a temporal ontological ground appears as a kind of horizon against which the correspondence of sentences with reality can assume a justified shape.

. . . the coordination of all knowing activity with what is known is not based on the fact that they are essentially the same [as Dilthey thought for the case of history; much less that they are formally the same, as logical positivists thought] but draws its significance from the particular nature of the mode of being that is common to both of them. It consists in the fact that neither the knower nor the known are present-at-hand in an 'ontic' way, but in a 'historical' one, i.e., they are of the mode of being of historicalness [temporality]. [*TM,* p. 232]

The flow of existence itself, then, is a disclosure of meanings. It is the fundamental deciphering or hermeneutical agency which then itself requires elucidation. This agency lies prior to such mental acts as issue in theories, hypotheses, and explanations, in the way that being precedes beings, truth precedes truths, and the task of philosophical hermeneutics precedes that of philological hermeneutics or of methodology generally.

It follows, as one can see, that for Gadamer hermeneutics exposes a field for universal reflection. It applies not only to the field of the human sciences but also to that of the natural sciences and even to our informal conversations with one another—anywhere, in short, that meanings appear. It is, in fact, the field of philosophy itself—"fundamental philosophy," in Aristotle's sense of the term.

But this presents the reader of *Truth and Method* with a certain puzzle in the interpretation of Gadamer's own work. If hermeneutics is a universal task, why does Gadamer devote the first two parts of *Truth and Method* (more than half the work) to an analysis of the hermeneutical phenomenon in the fields of art and historiography—why this narrower focus?

Part of the answer lies in Gadamer's pragmatic desire to counter the extension of scientific methods into the area of human sciences, but this is more like a motive for what he does than a reason for him to do it. The question becomes, what is there in the analysis of the aesthetic and historical experience which, in Gadamer's view, throws an especially clear and privileged light upon the hermeneutical phenomenon generally? This is not an easy question to answer, but the effort of finding an answer is valuable for our understanding of

Gadamer's position. If we expand a bit our consideration of Gadamer's notion of truth, we will have a better chance of answering this question. Toward this end, let us pause here on one aspect of Gadamer's notion of truth—its "productive" aspect. The gist of his thesis is made clear in the analysis he offers of the "hermeneutical relevance of Aristotle" (*TM,* pp. 278 ff., 471–472).

"Criticizing the Platonic idea of the good as an empty generality," writes Gadamer, "[Aristotle] asks instead the question of the humanly good, what is good in terms of human action" (*TM,* p. 278). Answering the question of the 'what is' does not answer the question of the 'what should be.' Yet the two questions are not divorced in the way that empiricism typically divides descriptive from prescriptive statements. A corrective of both extremes—the Platonist one that knowledge equals virtue, and the empiricist one that knowledge is not logically connected with virtue—is found in Aristotle. Besides a noetic element, knowledge inherently proclaims normative and productive ones as well.

Actually, the first two are already present in the empiricist understanding of truth, though "normative" may there function only in terms of a legislative model procedure to be imitated, not in moral terms. It is the "productive" or "applicable" aspect of knowledge that especially brings out Gadamer's position (cf. *TM,* pp. 274 ff.).

Aristotle asks whether the moral man uses his knowledge about himself and about society in the way that a craftsman uses his. The answer is yes, in some ways. The first thing is that it doesn't count as knowledge unless it is applied. The movement from reality to practice, however—and this is a second point—is far from unproblematic: there is resistance in reality to the application of the knowledge. The craftsman, Aristotle says, needs "luck," adding that luck comes more frequently to those who have minds prepared to recognize it. Moral knowledge, we may say, is like the technical knowledge of the craftsman in that it contains theoretical knowledge of a conceptual sort plus a practical knowledge and skill in applying the concepts to particular circumstances.

All the same, moral knowledge is very different from the craftsman's knowledge. The craftsman, for example, may have a guiding idea or plan when he sets out to build a house. In building it, he may well find that he has to adapt his idea to unforeseen resistances in his site and materials. Though these resistances may exercise and perfect his skills, however, they do not enrich his guiding idea.

It is otherwise with the application of a moral idea. Take the case of applying a law. The judge adapts himself to the circumstances of the case not for reasons of expediency or utility "but because to do otherwise would not be right" (*TM,* p. 284). It is the resistant circumstances of the case that bring out what the law is trying to say. They modify knowledge not so much of the way in which the law may be *applied* but of what the law *is.* This does not entail, as legal positivism holds, that the content of the law is pure convention, an induction from the customs and desires of the people. Aristotle contends that there is in natural law something that is beyond convention. But here, in a view that challenges interpretations frequently given

Aristotle, Gadamer argues that Aristotle's "natural" law is changeable—in this sense, that the content of its own nature exists "in a necessary tension with definite action, in that it is general and hence cannot contain within itself practical reality in its full concrete form" (*TM,* p. 284). Its imperfection, which creates the space for its modification (or, more accurately, for its coming to self-disclosure), lies not in itself but in the imperfect knowledge men have of it. In itself it is a nature or ideality that "constantly asserts itself," but not in the same way that fire, as Aristotle says, "burns everywhere in the same way, whether in Greece or in Persia" (cited in *TM,* p. 285). Gadamer says that Aristotle's "natural law" performs a "critical" function, not a dogmatic one, and that appeal to it is "legitimate only where a discrepancy emerges between one law and another" (ibid.). In this we see "a fundamental modification of the conceptual relation between means and ends, which distinguishes moral from technical knowledge" (*TM,* p. 286). Moral knowledge requires a special dimension of self-deliberation, for the "consideration of the means is itself a moral consideration and makes specific the moral rightness of the dominant end" (*TM,* p. 287). Hence, moral knowledge "can never be knowable in advance in the manner of a knowledge that can be taught" (*TM,* p. 287).

The problem with which Gadamer starts in this section is the problem of the movement between the general and the particular. It is a problem of understanding and, though it surely involves technique, it is not dissolved in technical considerations. The other hermeneuticists mentioned here could be enlisted on his side, however much their analyses differ from his. Belief in the validity of the sciences, as von Wright argues, rests conceptually upon belief in the validity of action. Von Wright concedes that this supposes a wider language community of practices and purposes (see *EU,* pp. 114–115, 147 ff.); that the validity of a practical syllogism does not require that the agent know exactly what he needs to do (cf. *EU,* p. 103); and that, especially in teleological explanations, volitional as well as cognitive elements go together (ibid.). The case in Habermas is even clearer: reason inheres in interest and not the other way around. This is, in fact, one of the points that Gadamer and Habermas have in common: truth is not contemplative at any level, and an account of knowing must not be such as to leave *theoria* and *praxis* in a state of estrangement, so that all that would be left would be either an instrumentalist movement from knowledge to application or a Nietzschean nihilistic resignation to life as an exercise of blind will (cf. *KI,* pp. 290 ff.). In Aristotle's analysis of movement from moral theory to moral practice, Gadamer holds, we have in capsule form "a kind of model of the problems of hermeneutics" (*TM,* p. 289). The "productive" element in truth, whose manner Aristotle describes in the *Ethics,* inheres in it everywhere: "application," writes Gadamer, "is an element of understanding itself" (*TM,* p. xx). "Application" brings out the "event-full" nature of understanding, its status as an ontological happening, and hence its difference in the world:

The meaning of application that is involved in all forms of understanding is now clear. It is not the subsequent applying to a concrete case of a given universal that we understand first by itself, but it is the actual understanding of the universal itself that the given text [or situation] constitutes for us. Understanding proves to be a kind of effect and knows itself as such. [*TM,* p. 305]

It follows that human knowing, like human existence, suffers from "thrownness," as Heidegger calls it—from coming to be in a situation of particularized and ongoing traditions, customs, and prejudices that deny to us the Cartesian possibility of freely adopting a place from which to begin our projects, whether those of thinking or of acting (cf. *TM,* pp. 234–235). Such a situation can never be completely illuminated, not because of imperfections in our methods but because of the finiteness of our being. Hence, error, too, has its ground—which is nothingness. Gadamer, in undertaking to compose a philosophical hermeneutics, is also in such a situation, which, like the test case for Aristotelian law, offers the possibility of enrichment precisely where resistances surface:

We are always within the situation, and to throw light on it is a task that is never entirely completed. This is also true of the hermeneutic situation, i.e. the situation in which we find ourselves with regard to the tradition we are trying to understand. . . . To exist historically means that knowledge of oneself can never be complete. All self-knowledge proceeds from what is historically pre-given, what we call, with Hegel, 'substance,' because it is the basis of all subjective meaning and attitude and hence both prescribes and limits every possibility of understanding any tradition whatsoever in terms of its unique historical quality. This almost defines the aim of philosophical hermeneutics: its task is to move back along the path of Hegel's phenomenology of mind until we discover in all that is subjective the substantiality that determines it. [*TM,* p. 269]

The difference is that Gadamer does not want to end in a disclosure of absolute mind or concept—in other words, in idealism—as Hegel does, but rather in a disclosure of being.

After this *excursus* on Gadamer's conception of truth, we can return to the question with which we began: Why does he focus on aesthetics and historiography when he is really asking about the general appearance of truth in experience?

The reason is complex: it has an upper and a deeper level.

At the upper and more obvious level we may say this: it is especially in their art and in the historical accounts they give of themselves that societies "think" themselves, give an account of their ethos and purpose. Thus, these disciplines bring to special prominence the moral or productive qualities of a society— qualities that are usually obscured or neutralized in the objectivist approaches of the natural sciences. As bearers of the self-image and moral dimensions of a society, the fields of aesthetics and historiography—or the *Geisteswissenschaften* generally—deserve special attention.

This is, nevertheless, only a superficial answer to the question of why Gadamer focuses on aesthetics and history. If we said only this, we would be left with the idea that society's "thinking itself" is merely a kind of communal exercise of subjectivity; we would not be getting past Dilthey's point that man only understands what he makes. In other words, we would be left with the fallacious idea that the initiative lies wholly with man.

But something about our experience of these disciplines points us toward a deeper level. The fields of aesthetics and historiography are notorious for their resistance to treatment by objectivist procedures (see *TM,* pp. xii–xiii). As a result, they have been to a great extent abandoned by modern philosophy and subsumed under psychology or sociology, which further consecrates the subjectivist view of these disciplines. But, if Gadamer is right, there is double fault here. Part of it is the failure to appreciate the aesthetic and historical phenomena for what they really are: not exercises purely of subjective initiative but events where truth—in the way that Aristotle spoke of natural law—asserts its resistance to subjectivist circumstances. The initiative in such a disclosure of truth does not lie wholly with ourselves: it arises "behind our backs," in a phrase from Hegel used several times by Gadamer. The other part of the fault is the failure to have a philosophy that could give an account of this dimension of truth. The "irrationality" attributed by much of modern philosophy to these areas has its source not in the phenomena themselves but in the inability of much modern philosophy to face these phenomena with the right questions, to practice about them "right reasoning," in Aristotle's sense of the term. There are, of course, historical grounds for this inability. Gadamer tries to show what they are. That is why, in the first two parts of *Truth and Method,* he

reviews at length the reflections of philosophers—
especially Kant and Dilthey—on aesthetic and historical experience. But his aim is not merely negative.
Even in these philosophers' limitations we can see
something happening "over and above their wanting
and doing." His method is dialectical, Socratic, prob-
ing but listening at the same time. In this portion of his
work, Gadamer is simply paralleling the analyses of
Heidegger, whose insight into the forestructures of
understanding made him realize that he had to review
critically the "important turning points in the history
of metaphysics" (*TM,* p. 239). What Heidegger did
for metaphysics Gadamer is attempting to do for philosophies of aesthetics and of history. It is true that
Gadamer, like Heidegger, has a "forestructure" in his
mind before he begins this review—a prejudice, one
can say (about which more later)—but his aim, at
least, is to avoid imposing this dogmatically. He tries
to use it, rather, as a question addressed to the texts. If
the texts resist the question addressed to them, then his
own "forestructures" are exposed in their limitations.
If the texts respond in a new way to this new question,
then the historical limitations of the texts are overcome. In either case, one has the chance of gaining
"right understanding from the things themselves"
(ibid.).

In our second point, then, we turn to Gadamer's
"questioning" of the things themselves as they are
reflected in the texts of Kant and Dilthey. This will not
be simply a matter of offering a historical, in the sense
of objectivist, account of Kant and Dilthey. It is an
interpretation, made in the light of Heidegger's notion
of truth.

Kant and Dilthey
on Philosophies of
Aesthetics and History

Taking a starting point from the eighteenth century, let us consider for the sake of brevity the philosophies of aesthetics and of history together. They reveal a common limitation under different appearances, like varying sides of a coin that share the same substance. The differences are these: philosophies of aesthetics tend to become accounts of the history of taste, with a consequent devaluation of the concept of value; philosophies of history tend to become accounts of the history of ideas, with a consequent devaluation of the concept of truth. As a result, the connection between values and ideas is diminished. The substantial error in both cases is the defective role assigned to the subject who, however, is the one who sustains both thought and values. Kant and Dilthey, as the most prominent representatives of the two tendencies, illustrate the case.

Kant's aesthetics is subjectivist, though it offers no basis for the extreme subjectivism of, Gadamer holds, a later Valéry or Lukács. These held that the artistic work is indifferent to the interpretations given it by the viewer (Valéry) or that, lacking unity completed in itself, it is only the occasion for eliciting a unity in the experience of the viewer (Lukács) (see *TM,* pp. 84 – 85). Kant's subject, in contrast, is a synthesizer who unifies the plurality of impressions, whether he does this at the moment of creating a work (the point that Valéry leaves unilluminated) or at the moment of its viewing (the point that Lukács inadequately explores).

Kant recognized an a priori in the artistic act, and yet he is the father of subjectivism. How did this come to pass?

In the *Critique of Practical Reason,* Kant had argued that the validity of a moral norm entails its being abstractable from subjective conditions of satisfaction so that it could be held by humanity everywhere. Disinterestedness was the essence of a norm's transcendental worth. Nothing less than that could suffice as a basis for communal moral judgments.

The beautiful, however, is precisely that which gives individual pleasure. Interest inheres in its essence. This feature seems to preclude, therefore, the elevation of the experience of beauty to a transcendental status. But that would mean that no foundation could be given for communal judgments in matters of taste and beauty, and also that no moral judgments could be passed on the beautiful. It is clear, Kant holds, that taste and the pleasure of the beautiful are not the results of acts of reflection or of conceptualization. Such conceptualizations, if they existed, could be taught. If so, a community could acquire, as it does in the field of arithmetic, the correct rules of procedure for deciding questions of taste and beauty (cf. *TM,* p. 36). But, on the other hand, the community of judgment that we do in fact find in society is not arrived at by induction, by noting what people do consider "good taste" or "beautiful." It is the nature of aesthetic judgments, Kant holds, not to say that people *will* agree with one's judgment (that may be true but is not the point) but that they *should* agree with it. Kant finds himself committed, then, to finding in the experience of the beautiful an a priori that can be the basis for "communal pleasure," so to call it, but which is at the same time not a conceptualization (cf. *TM,* p. 48). In the aesthetic experience, "no knowledge of the object will be imparted" (*TM,* p. 41), but at the same time an ideality must be present which somehow abstracts from all subjective and private conditions. Kant solves his problem with considerable ingenuity.

The model experience is that of the beautiful in nature, which presents itself to us immediately, without the mediation of concepts, and which gives pleasure of itself, without taking account of our subjective ends and purposes: "natural beauty . . . possesses no significance of content, and thus manifests the judgment of taste in its unintellectualized purity" (*TM,* p. 46; cf. p. 43). It is an end in itself.

What does art, "non-natural" beauty, add to this? It adds the example of the ideality of natural beauty being taken up and given a fresh presentation through the free play of imaginative action. This is the action of genius, the "capacity to represent aesthetic ideas" (*TM,* p. 48). What genius expresses, however, is not just the ideality of a tree or a horse or a flower, but of man himself, in a moment of free play that revivifies the free play of nature's own forces. Genius in this is precisely different from the academician's or pedant's "rigid adherence to rules" (*TM,* p. 49). Rules can be taught. "The art of genius is to make the free play of the mental faculties available" (ibid.). In the artistic object, therefore, man recognizes something both of his and of nature's free self, devoid of rules, concepts, and deliberate purposes. It is this presence of imaginative ideality afforded by genius that is the a priori basis for the pleasure we experience in the presence of the beautiful. Such genius, to repeat the point, is not at the disposal of training. It cannot be learned. It is its own beginning and its own end.

"Art is art created by genius" means that for artistic beauty also [i.e., besides natural beauty] there is no other principle of judgment, no criterion of concept and knowledge, than that of its finality for the feeling of freedom in the play of our cognitive faculties. Beauty in nature or art has the same a priori principle, which lies entirely within subjectivity. The autonomy of aesthetic judgment does not mean that there is an autonomous sphere of validity for beautiful objects. Kant's transcendental reflection on the a priori of judgment justifies the claim of the aesthetic judgment for a community of judgment, but basically it does not permit a philosophical aesthetics in the sense of a philosophy of art. [*TM,* p. 51]

This result in the *Critique of Judgment* is, of course, completely consistent with the doctrine of the other two *Critiques,* which show how the concept of knowledge applies to the theoretical and practical uses of reason. The *Critique of Judgment,* by showing that the universality of aesthetic judgment neither rests on nor calls for a theoretical elaboration, effectively sets the outer boundary to the sphere of reliable knowledge. On the one side of it, the side of the first two *Critiques,* lie considerations of truth; on the other, the side of aesthetic judgments, lie considerations of "taste," "feeling," and so on.

This thesis, in Gadamer's judgment, marked a turning point of incalculable consequence for the cultural sciences. After Kant, these had no recourse but to seek to base their claims to truth—if they still wanted to make them—on the same grounds as did the natural sciences, or to give up the search for a philosophical base entirely. In the latter case, the loss could be made easier, perhaps, by consigning to them the residues of "artistic elements," "feeling," and "empathy" in experience. In either case, the possibility of their making a unique philosophical contribution to the history of man's quest for truth and understanding was foreclosed (cf. *TM,* pp. 38–39). And yet it is in the fields especially studied by the human sciences that the ideals of culture, education, national purpose, communal cohesion, and so on, are chiefly transmitted. These are all exercises in intersubjectivity. Kant, however, left intersubjectivity in a state in which it could only be conceptually explored in the methods proper to the logic of the natural sciences. "Is it," Gadamer asks, in a question analogous to that of Habermas, "right [i.e., "right thinking"] to reserve the concept of truth for conceptual knowledge? Must we not also admit that the work of art possesses truth?" (*TM,* p. 39). In the positive portion of his work, he will try to show how this is so.

Kant's thesis had its effects not only on philosophies of aesthetics but also on those of history. His conception of genius was taken up by Dilthey in the notion of *Erlebnis.*

'Experience' meant two things: immediacy and totality (cf. *TM,* pp. 55 ff.). 'Immediacy' indicates that meanings are present without the need for a process of ratiocination. 'Totality' means that the content of the meaning has weight and significance enough to unify the myriad moments of a person's life. 'Experience' viewed like this is the primary datum of historical research. In autobiography, the datum appears in its purest form. Only the individual who is the possessor of such an experience can relate it in its immediacy and totality. But it takes a genius to see such meanings in his life and to express them. In this way, 'experience' as embedded in the historical text became the analogue to science's object embedded in the behavior of nature. And Dilthey's philosophy of history, Gadamer argues, became the other face of Kant's philosophy of art.

Where Kant resolved aesthetic experience into the synthesizing role of the subjective judgment, Dilthey resolved historical experience into the objectified presentation, chiefly in texts, of subjective meanings. Kant grounded the communality of aesthetic pleasure on the presence in aesthetic experience of an a priori of ideal beauty—that is, the presence in sensuous form of the free play of the imagination. Dilthey based the communality of historical meanings on the a priori of conaturality between self-meanings and the meanings of other selves as present in symbols, the "objectified mind" of Hegel.

But there is a difference, too. Kant's illumination of aesthetic experience was, so to speak, self-contained and ended with the experience, without appealing to a wider context of explanation. Dilthey, influenced (as Kant was also, in fact, but not to the same effect) by the procedures of the natural sciences, relied finally on a version of these to secure the objectivity of historical experience. This came about because Dilthey's a priori, the conaturality of intentions, was an interpenetration of "life-structures." Hence, even the under-

standing of another's text was a form of self-understanding. A doubt arising about the text was also a
doubt arising in self-understanding. Gadamer quotes
Dilthey: "Consciousness has shaken off authority and
is seeking through reflection and doubt to attain to
valid knowledge" (*TM*, p. 210). "The Cartesian
echoes cannot be missed," Gadamer adds. Dilthey his-
toricizes Descartes.

But, Gadamer continues, this introduces a contradiction in Dilthey's own project of offering a foundation for the human sciences. It is "life," Dilthey had
said, "[that] is able to assert itself against [doubt]"
(ibid.). On the one hand, Dilthey appeals to a Cartesian reflection that implies the adoption of an "external" point of view and of some sort of historical version of the *Discourse on Method* to secure the "traditions
of morals, religion, and positive law which are in dan-
ger of being destroyed by reflection and need a new
order" (ibid.). On the other hand, he acknowledges
that these traditions are the sedimentation of a self-
knowledge immanent in them and must be, if they are
to survive, somehow self-verifying (in the sense earlier mentioned of a meaning that "constantly asserts
itself" against resistances). Dilthey fails to distinguish
between methodological doubt, in the deliberate Cartesian fashion, and doubts that come (in the resistance
of circumstances) of their own accord. He leaves no
room for the latter. "The certainty of science is, for
him, the culminating form of the certainty of life"
(*TM*, p. 211). He fails to acknowledge (faithful in this
to Kant) the possibility of different modes of certainty.
Gadamer concludes:

We shall readily grant Dilthey that the influence of thought on life "comes from the inner need to fix something firm in the restless change of sense impressions, desires and feelings, something that enables one's life to be steady and unified." But this achievement in thought is something immanent in life itself and takes place in the objectifications of the mind, morals, law, and religion, which support the individual insofar as he surrenders himself to the objectivity of society. The fact that it is necessary to adopt the "attitude of reflection and doubt" and that this is what happens "in all forms of scientific reflection" (and not otherwise) simply cannot be combined with Dilthey's life philosophy. This is, rather, a description of the special ideal of the scientific enlightenment, which is as little compatible with a reflection immanent in life as the "intellectualism" of the enlightenment was, against which Dilthey's grounding in the fact of the philosophy of life was directed. [*TM,* p. 210]

One could, therefore, conclude that Dilthey's project of complementing Kant's two *Critiques* with a "critique of historical consciousness" pushed him farther than he wanted to go. Like Kant in the case of art, Dilthey in the case of history made it impossible for the human sciences to find, at least in his versions of philosophy, a foundation for their unique contribution to the history of truth.

Gadamer's historical questioning of the texts reveals that both Kant's philosophy of art and Dilthey's philosophy of history found a basis for intersubjectivity, but at too high a price. In Kant it is a unique basis (not homogeneous with that of science) but one that is beyond further conceptual justification. In Dilthey it is a basis that offers a promise of justification but only in methods that would destroy its uniqueness. Guided, then, negatively by the limitations in Kant and Dilthey, and positively by Heidegger's ontology of the forestructures of understanding, Gadamer tries to show that our experiences of art and of history respond to a different synthesis of the role of subject and object, one that does not fracture the givenness of truth as at the same time noetic, normative, and productive. His phenomenology of game-playing reveals this in the case of aesthetics, and his discussion of tradition does the same for the case of history. Our third section takes up these two positive developments.

Gadamer's Phenomenology
of Game-playing
and Discussion of Tradition

In Gadamer's phenomenology of game-playing two notable characteristics are revealed.

First, the player surrenders his separate stance and is absorbed into the movement of the game. His individual projects are suspended, not so much at the point where he decides to enter the game but, more significantly, within the actual playing itself. There the movement of the game "takes from him the burden of the initiative" (*TM,* p. 94). It would be truer to say that the game plays the players than that the players play the game (cf. *TM,* p. 96).

Secondly, though the game cannot be played without players, its nature is not exhausted in their playing. The game has rules and a structure of its own. When played, these take actual shape but never exactly the same shape. No game is simply a repetition of a previous game. It would be more accurate to say that an actual game is a re-presentation of this structure. It re-presents but never repeats the past. No game is exhausted in any single play. It can be entirely taken up again as though it had not happened before: it "has no goal which brings it to an end; rather it renews itself in constant repetition" (*TM,* p. 93). A special mode of temporality is revealed, then, in the phenomenon of game-playing. A structure, at first sight atemporal, is actuated but not categorically captured in temporal play.

At this point ('play' suggests as much), one might expect Gadamer to say that the game is an analogue of art. He goes further than this. He says, "human play finds its true perfection in being art, 'the transformation into structure'" (*TM,* p. 99). Art is the ideal of play. This is an echo of Kant's insight that connected art with freedom. The ideality of play finds a purer form in art. Aesthetic experience is an absorption of the artist or viewer into a movement that suspends his deliberately adopted attitudes and purposes. It "becomes an experience changing the person experiencing it" (*TM,* p. 92). Art, like the game, is not an object that the subject controls by attitudes, techniques, or rules. Its fascination for the participant derives precisely from its autonomy.

Yet the autonomy is not unlimited. Art, again like the game, has its practitioners, a time, and a place. It is always "for someone" (*TM,* p. 99): "representation must be recognized as the mode of the being of the work of art" (*TM,* p. 104). In representing a structure, art fulfills a "clear cognitive function" (*TM,* p. 103) and does not consist primarily in the sensuous enjoyment of the free. Free play in art is "subject to the supreme criterion of the 'right' representation" (*TM*, p. 106).

This is the place to pause and explain what Gadamer means by that word 'right,' which has also occurred in an earlier passage cited, where Gadamer used the term "right thinking."

Gadamer is not using the word as a methodologist does. For a methodologist, 'right' connotes an ideal standard consciously espoused, which the research is meant to approximate. For example, a researcher might hold that the 'right' interpretation of a text or of a ritual practice is the sense that the author had in mind in writing the text or the meaning that the society attributes to the practice of its ritual.

Gadamer does not deny the utility of this sense of 'right,' but it is not his special meaning in *Truth and Method*. 'Right' for him, we may perhaps say, connotes something of what we mean in our usage of the phrase 'civil rights,' but in a sense that precedes explicit custom or court-enforced laws. It is basically the sense indicated by Jefferson's phrase "inalienable rights," which do not await the enactment of statutes to make themselves felt. It is a kind of understanding in man that calls for recognition and resists suppression. It is not simply a matter of will, of pure desire, but a matter of informed will. 'Right' connotes a nucleus of understanding that exercises a critical function. This is how Gadamer can say that rightness is recognized in the fact that "what now exists, what represents itself in the play of art, is what is lasting and true" (*TM*, p. 100).

Note that we do not know in advance what this rightness consists in. It does not subsist as a rule which one can methodically apply. In Jefferson's apparent sense of the phrase, it is not "self-evident." It is a nucleus in man's mental life which presents a resistance to changing conditions and it is this resistance to or questioning by circumstances that gradually allows its truthfulness to become clear. The circumstances are a "re-presentation" of this nucleus, whether in the world of drama or in that of alternative political forms. It is not a nucleus available to research at the methodologist's level. It only manifests itself in being reexperienced. Gadamer's comments on Aristotle's definition of tragedy help explain what he means (cf. *TM,* pp. 114 ff.).

The tragic play both arouses and heals the spectator's distress. The spectator is horrified to see that reality can be like this and is torn within himself by an inner rebellion against this revelation. But the play also shows that there is something truly common in this excess of suffering and that a form of genuine communion is made available to the spectator. There is peace, finally, in the recognition that this is "how it is," and the spectator gains in self-knowledge.

Can one ask 'right' in another way than this? Yes, of course one can. One may for special purposes wish to single out the noetic or structural aspect of the work. Still, one must be wary even there. It both does and does not make sense to ask whether there is one 'right' painting of Notre Dame or one 'right' interpretation of *Hamlet* (just as it makes no sense to ask whether there is one 'right' way to play a game). The objectivist sciences perform a useful role in telling us what Shakespeare meant by such-and-such a line, but they do not tell us whether we can share in such a meaning, nor why *Hamlet* survives though other plays equally invested with Elizabethan meanings do not. This, which is the essence of artistic quality, can only be tested in re-presentation; it cannot be researched. The special temporality of the game, at once timeless and timely, finds its apotheosis in the temporality of art. The advantage of art over the game is that the temporality of *understanding* shows up in a supreme way in the play of art (cf. *TM,* p. 63).

But this does not perhaps happen in the way most frequently encountered. Much more common to us in our daily experience is the effort to fill, by understanding, the gaps between ourselves and our past, or between ourselves and other cultures. To facilitate this is the aim of the historical sciences. How does the temporality of understanding function in these disciplines?

No one, in fact, approaches a historical document in a purely neutral way. He has in him the patternings instilled by his own tradition and culture. These are "prejudices" *(Vorurteile)* which, even more than our judgments deliberately reached, "constitute the historical reality" of one's own being (*TM,* p. 245). These lead an interpreter to have certain expectations with regard to the meaning of a text. But even if the interpreter makes allowances for his own biases, he still, in actually reading a text, "projects before himself a meaning for the text as a whole as soon as some initial meaning emerges in the text" (*TM,* p. 266). Interpreting, then, institutes a circular movement between the interpreter's expectations and the meanings residing within the text. These limiting "forestructures" are the prejudices that work toward understanding. "This recognition that all understanding inevitably involves some prejudice gives the hermeneutical problem its real thrust" (*TM,* p. 239).

But, since the Enlightenment, 'prejudice' has been given a purely pejorative status. Even the advocates and protectors of religious traditions, though they felt themselves lucky to have the "right" prejudices, were enough influenced by the ethos of the Enlightenment to seek to base their beliefs upon proofs of an objectivist sort. Against this "prejudice against 'prejudice,'" Gadamer defends the concept of a "legitimate prejudice," that is, of the idea that a prejudice is not only not an obstacle but can also be a positive aid to understanding (see *TM,* p. 240). What can be the grounds for the legitimacy of prejudice?

Once again, the key element is the temporality of understanding. One thinks of the historian as setting a distance between himself and his text, of fixing it in standards of authenticity, accuracy, relationship to other texts, and so on. This is what objectivist methods decree. But this means that a gap is supposed and consecrated between the interpreter's own tradition and those that are present in a text's expression. Its individual and monadic sense might be captured in such methods but not its serious manifestation of objective truth for life—in other words, not its "productive" aspect.

The temporal distance between the interpreter and the text might offer a better result. It might let "the true meaning of the object emerge fully" (*TM,* p. 265). For this to happen, one must be prepared to face his own prejudices, his "expectations of meaning," to face the risk of their being exposed as groundless. Here too, then, the initiative of the interpreter would be partially taken from his hands. The text itself must be allowed to put a question to the interpreter. Not the question "What did I here, as a past author and different individual, have in mind when I wrote this?" but rather "What truth shows up if my 'prejudices' and yours confront each other on the occasion of this text?" "Not occasionally only," writes Gadamer, "but always, the meaning of a text goes beyond its author. That is why understanding is not merely a reproductive, but always a productive attitude as well" (*TM,* p. 264). This, too, is Socrates's point, taking issue with the sophistic thesis defended by Cratylus that there is no difference between the truth-function of speech and the significant character of words. Socrates's dedication to dialectic is absolute not because he lacks linguistic skills but because "*logos,* speech, and utterance, and the revelation of objects that takes place in it, is something different from the intending of the meanings contained in words, and that the actual capacity of language to communicate what is correct and true is founded on the former" (*TM,* p. 372). This is why, in Gadamer's view, there may be ambiguities, even inconsistencies, in the work of a great philosopher or historian: "it is the nature of a dialogue that is directed towards an object [reality] to risk illogicality" (*TM,* p. 489). Thus the dialectic, or hermeneutical circle in the form Heidegger gave it, is not a methodological device; it "describes an ontological structural element in understanding" (*TM,* p. 261). We do, of course, in interpreting a text, want to identify our own prejudice. But how can we do this? "It is impossible to make ourselves aware of it while it is constantly operating unnoticed, but only when it is, so to speak, stimulated.

The encounter with a text from the past can provide this stimulus" (*TM,* p. 266). This is the most palpable contribution of the text's temporal distance. It lets the prejudices wither that are unproductive and revivifies those that, in their resistance to change, bring about a better understanding of the real. "Understanding begins . . . when something addresses us. This is the primary hermeneutical condition. We now know what this requires, namely the fundamental suspension of our own prejudices. But all suspension of judgments and hence, a fortiori, of prejudices, has logically the structure of a question" (*TM,* p. 266).

There are echoes of Descartes here, but they are not methodological. Gadamer, in his concept of prejudice suspended, finds no freely chosen point from which to begin. He does not suppose that truth is timeless. More significantly, there are echoes of Dilthey, for Dilthey, too, saw that in the historical sciences the interpreter is part of the flow he is attempting to understand. But Dilthey's ambivalence, which led him finally to give understanding refuge in objectivist methods, meant that his interpreter became, in the end, a contemplative who inspected the historical object from a distance. In methodologically becoming ahistorical himself, he lost the opportunity to let the historicality of thinking work, show itself as historical (cf. *TM,* p. 213). What Gadamer most clearly adds to Dilthey's historical datum is its "working" aspect, the nature of history as "effective-history" *(Wirkungsgeschichte).* Awareness of this working aspect he calls "effective-historical consciousness" *(wirkungsgeschichtliches Bewußtsein).*

One must be careful to distinguish the consciousness Gadamer is talking about from that commonly urged on an interpreter, to the effect that he suspend his own biases, "try to see the other's point of view." This would be something that the interpreter *does*. If this were all that is meant, then the interpreter would simply be freezing both his object and himself into static patterns, with the result that the "effective-historical" nature of the historical datum could not be productive; the text (while perhaps admitted to be uttering something *intended*) would be "forced to abandon its claim that it is uttering something true" (*TM*, p. 270). And the interpreter would not realize that "effective-historical consciousness" is operating productively within his own act of understanding. It is operative precisely in his "choice of the right question to ask" (*TM*, p. 268).

Regarded from a methodical point of view, the consciousness that Gadamer is talking about is one that does not make the interpreter's own standpoint "safely unattainable" (*TM*, p. 270). The ontological basis for this recommendation is the Heideggerian thesis that our situation, the horizon we occupy, has its own past and future, independently both of ourselves and of the text or culture we wish to understand, for neither of us chose them by intentional act. The attainment of understanding is actually a "fusing of horizons," an event in which what seemed to be frontiers dividing two horizons vanishes, so that only one human community of thought and action remains. Sometimes this fusion of horizons can take place without our noticing it, especially in the experience of great art. It happens, as it were, "behind our back," and we realize it in deliberate consciousness only afterward. It is such an event, Gadamer holds, that shows, beyond our purposes ("wanting") and our adoption of means ("doing"), the fact or being of "effective-historical consciousness."

Now we can see more clearly why Gadamer chose aesthetics and history as the paradigm fields for analysis in his ontological version of truth. We experience the aesthetic object and the historical object—our tradition or culture—in an immediate and totalizing way and not by the adoption of a conceptual calculus or technique. Not, at least, *originally* by the adoption of such means, though we may afterwards in conscious reflection return to this experience in a methodical way. "Effective-historical consciousness" reveals itself more clearly in the experience of the aesthetic and historical objects than it does in the objects of natural science.

The fact that our horizon of effective understanding is not one that we consciously acquire, but is rather an ongoing act of understanding, indicates that we need a horizon "in order to be able to place ourselves within a situation" (*TM,* p. 271). Understanding, therefore, is a question neither of holding another's horizon at arm's length, in an objectivist manner, nor of empathic fusion with another horizon, in a psychologistic manner. Both of these "consciousnesses" maintain the fiction that there can be a totally "other" horizon. On the contrary,

In the process of understanding there takes place a real fusing of horizons, which means that as the historical horizon is projected, it is simultaneously removed. We described the conscious act of this fusion as the task of the effective-historical consciousness. . . . it is, in fact, the central problem of hermeneutics. It is the problem of application that exists in all understanding. [*TM,* pp. 273–274].

The Linguistic Nature of Experience

The horizons mentioned in the previous section, therefore, are structures that effectively enclose us. We experience a certain passivity within them. We did not freely adopt them, nor can we freely get outside them. But these structures at the same time make variation and expansion possible. They give us a point of view from which differences and variation can be triggered and recognized. They have something of the character of finished structures, like statements, but at the same time something of the character of probes, like questions. This last feature becomes especially prominent when one of our settled horizons makes contact with another horizon very different from it, as happens when we make contact with another culture or have to translate a foreign language.

There is a suggestion in all this that these horizons function like language, which also effectively encloses us but at the same time makes the perception and the creation of meaning possible. If one carried this suggestion through, one would conclude that understanding at the effective level discussed by Gadamer has a linguistic character. Gadamer takes this step. "We emphasized that the experience of meaning which takes place in understanding always includes application. Now we are to note that this whole process is linguistic" (*TM,* p. 345).

Gadamer remarks that Wittgenstein's concept of language games seemed "quite natural" to him (*TM,* p. 500 n. 12) when he came across it. He, like Wittgenstein, agrees that it is our language that gives us a world, not as an instrument which we deliberately use to carve a world, but as an activity in which language and world first appear (cf. Gadamer 1976, p. 126). But Wittgenstein, in his concern to avoid any postulate of transcendental "game" or grammar, left the plurality of human language-games in isolation from one another and, apparently, relied on a behavioral repetition of the learning process in order to explain how someone could learn another's language-game (cf. Gadamer 1976, Linge's introduction, p. xxxvii; cf. Apel 1976, p. 39). Gadamer, however, holds that even our first language-learning is not primarily, much less exclusively, a matter of our directing our attention (or of someone else's directing it)—which is what Wittgenstein suggests—but an event, a kind of drama, which puts objects "on the scale of words" (*TM,* p. 359). In this sense the actually shaped word is an image or symbol and not a sign conventionally determined. Consequently, one's initial learning of a language is a learning, not only of some particular language, but of what language-learning itself is. As Linge puts it in his introduction, "Learning our first language and learning subsequent ones are not the same thing. . . . [In] learning the first language, we acquire the basis for altering it and fusing it with other language games" (Gadamer 1976, p. xxxviii). There is, then, Linge goes on to say, a Hegelian influence on Gadamer which is missing in Wittgenstein. Yet Gadamer agrees with Wittgenstein, and against Hegel, on the rejection of any transcendent language or grammar or absolute mind.

When Gadamer writes, "The linguistic nature of this bringing into language is the same as that of the human experience of the world in general" (*TM,* p. 414), the reader is tempted to take this thesis of the universality of language to mean that language, whether in the more strict sense of speech or in the looser one of gesture, facial expressions, institutions, and the like, is simply the everywhere-present medium of our socialization, and the medium we then take up ourselves in order to express ourselves. This seems essentially to be Habermas's meaning: language itself is a kind of sedimented ideology which must be critiqued so that the corrupt forms residing in its usage can be detected. Habermas, Gadamer says, takes the function of language as "re-productive"—that is, as giving expression to a structure consciously or unconsciously ingested in the speaker and which may or may not be a corrupt structure (cf. *TM,* Supplement II, p. 493). Gadamer does not deny that a given language may function this way and so need critiquing. But this is not his meaning. For him, language is not fundamentally an act giving expression to a preexisting structure. It is not in this sense "re-productive." It is, in a way much closer to Wittgenstein's thought, "productive." His critique of the prejudice against prejudice, where one sees prejudice as purely negative and restrictive, applies here. The fundamental being of language is the "presumption of meaning in general" together with the "explicit determination of what one

presumed" (*TM,* Supplement II, p. 497). One's finding words for his thought is an "explicit determination," but it is not a tool-usage: one's "determination"
does not have that note of mastery in it; one finds, in
assuming a word, that "you are fixed in a direction of
thought which comes from afar and stretches beyond
you" (*TM,* p. 496).

Gadamer illustrates his thought by noting the con-
trasting ways in which we experience language when
we are translating and when we are freely expressing
ourselves (cf. Gadamer 1976, pp. 86–87; 65–68). In
the former case we feel hemmed in by the demands of
the foreign tongue. We are very conscious of groping
for the right word. We keep checking our efforts
against the demands of the foreign text. But when we
are freely expressing ourselves—this is especially noticeable when the topic is one we feel deeply about—it
is as though we try to get away from a conscious
choosing of terms and try, instead, to let our unshaped
thoughts find their own expression. It is as though we
wanted to bring it about that language speak through us.

Hence, Gadamer sides with Plato and against Cratylus when Plato argues that the "soul's interior dialogue
with itself" is not something that can be done at the
level of words. Still, Plato, too, is wrong in supposing
that there is an ideal system of signs which gives words
what power they have (cf. *TM,* pp. 366–375). This
would leave unanswered the real problem of the relations between words and things. St. Thomas Aquinas
has a better thesis. Guided by the Christian notion of
the *logos* made flesh, he realizes that the *logos* can be
freed from its Platonist spirituality and become historical, "pure event" (*TM,* p. 379). Aquinas applies this

seminal insight to the case of man's forming a universal concept and uses the image of a mirror, which Gadamer also adopts, to explain his thesis.

"The word is like a mirror in which the object is seen. The curious thing about this mirror, however, is that it nowhere extends beyond the image of the object" (*TM*, p. 384). This particular mirror exhausts itself in its act of representing. Whatever imperfections inhere in it distort perhaps—but we don't know it from the mirroring itself—the object or reality coming to view.

The mirroring function—not this or that particular reflection—is what Gadamer means by the "linguisticality" of man. The word itself is chosen because, say, better than Aristotle's term "political" or Hegel's term "mind" or Dilthey's term "historical consciousness," it expresses the nature of man as the active or productive place where reality appears as objects. All semantics, creativity, interpretation are based on this ontological datum. "Being that can be understood," says Gadamer in a phrase that has become the emblem of his thesis, "is language" (*TM*, p. 432).

Another image helps to make his point clearer (cf. *TM*, p. 439). He takes up an ancient theme, the analogy of truth with light. Light itself is not seen but only as reflected from the surface on which it plays. "Light," we might paraphrase, "which can be seen is surfaces." A particular man, a "situated" man (as a particular text), is a particular surface. The act of understanding is an event that involves a passivity of this sort (cf. *TM*, p. 422). Interpretation is the illumination of the act of understanding. It shows the true nature of effective-historical consciousness, namely, that it has "no tangible being of its own and yet [throws] back the image that is presented to it" (*TM*, p. 431). This combined note of passivity and of radiance of structure brings us back to the phenomenon of the game:

> What we mean by truth here can best be determined again in terms of our concept of play. . . . Language games are where we, as learners—and when do we cease to be that?—rise to the understanding of the world. . . . [It is] the game itself that plays in that it draws the players into itself and thus becomes the actual *subjectum* of the playing. What corresponds to this in the present case is neither play with language nor with the contents of the experience of the world or of tradition that speaks to us, but the play of language itself, which addresses us, proposes and withdraws, asks, and fulfills itself in the answer. [*TM*, p. 446]

The key to understanding Gadamer's position is to understand what he does with the Heideggerian notion of temporality. This hypothetical insight, which Heidegger put to the test in *Being and Time,* of its nature forbids a purely semantical, and *a fortiori* a purely formal, treatment. Only a descriptive approach to its elucidation is possible. But descriptive language is notoriously metaphorical. There is, however, no other way of tracing its effects while respecting its hypothesized original status. Perhaps the following extended metaphor may help clarify Gadamer's position.

Suppose two people, otherwise strangers, are sitting close to each other on the grass outside a classroom building. *B* turns to *A* and asks, "What time do you have?" *A* consults his watch and answers, "It's five minutes to two."

A, let us suppose, is not himself interested in the time. He notes, because his attention has been called to it, the position of the hands on the face of his watch in the same spirit as he might note that there is a crack in the sidewalk or that there are swallows flying about. His noting of the time leads nowhere, has no connections, is isolated, atomic, unproductive. This is the most neutral sense of "clock-time."

But *B* has an important exam at two o'clock. This is a more important sense of clock-time, for a certain applicability or significance of clock-time has been taken up in one of *B*'s life projects. But this project is one that *B* deliberately adopted. He didn't have to, but he did, and from this decision clock-time assumes an importance it does not otherwise have.

Now suppose, sitting unnoticed not far away but within earshot, is *C. C* has learned a short time before that he has not long to live. The prospect of death makes *C* aware of an entirely different dimension of time. Time, for him, is the applicability of his life, of the project he had no say in launching, though it is the basis of all other projects. His being and his temporality are not just coterminous, in a calendrical sort of way, as are the duration of music from the portable radio and the life of the batteries which supply energy for its reproduction: they are the same thing.

Gadamer is saying that man's linguisticality is the same thing as his temporality. A person's native tongue is to him what the watch is to *A* and *B,* a sometimes idle, sometimes indispensable instrument. But silence, total silence, total inexpressiveness, would be to him what death is to *C.* "Language-ing," in this deeper sense, is the same as his living.

For Gadamer, then, language is time, is human existence, is being, is truth. It is the happening of everything meaningful, of everything "for us." Because we are "thrown into language" it happens "over and above our wanting and our doing." But, as in the case of playing a game, or in that of creating or appreciating an art object, or in that of composing or reading a history, it does not happen without us. An individual's "linguisticality" is the surface upon which truth plays, the only place it becomes visible. With this in mind, Gadamer has argued, one has a "truthful" control for the subsequent deployment of methods, as well as a philosophy for locating methods in their proper epistemological place. The negative task of philosophical hermeneutics was to show, against the pretensions of scientism, how the possibility of truth comes before and is supposed by the possibilities of method. The positive task was to show how the possibility of truth becomes real in the linguistic existence that is man.

Conclusion

It is time to draw some of these strings together. I would like to do this by adopting, so to call it, a "high-altitude" approach, pointing out certain of the more salient features of the hermeneutical landscape together with just a brief mention of some weaknesses and strengths.

Explanation and Understanding

Let us begin by recalling some general features of the relationship between explanation and understanding.

A first remark: our experience tells us that knowing something involves a variety of mental activities, strategies, and resolutions. One of the features common to our experience is a sense of settledness about the point in question, a kind of endorsed, though perhaps tentative, end put to the activity of inquiring about or reflecting about. We experience this, for example, when we say that if we know that A implies B and also that A, then we know that B; or, when we say that we know that if we eat these oysters we will have a painful rash by tomorrow; or, listening to someone discuss a political proposal, a personal problem, a movie, a championship game, when we say that we know what they mean (or 'see' what they mean, or 'understand' what they mean). Note that in these last examples it is not necessary that we agree with the point being made (or even feel good about it), in order to experience this sense of mental settledness.

If the above are accepted as examples of resolutions commonly arrived at in our mental puzzlements, we should note that the strategies used for reaching these resolutions are very different. The first two depend on deductive or inductive strategies. The last very often involves a discourse which looks more like a negotiation than anything else, where *A* says *'this'* and *B* says 'But what about *that?'* and *A* replies 'Well, but *this* fits better with *this* and *this'* and so on and *B* finally says 'Well, yes, now I see what you mean' and maybe adds '. . . though I'm still not sure I agree.' It is plain that the first two strategies cluster around the pole of knowing we call 'explanation' and the third around the pole called 'understanding.'

Let us for the sake of argument accept this rough distinction in epistemological foci and, in a second step, ask abstractly what possible relationships could exist between these two poles. We use the following table to illustrate the cases, where 'yes' admits a distinctive and competent range of knowing and 'no' denies such a range:

	Column A Explanation	*Column B* Understanding
(1)	Yes	Yes
(2)	Yes	No
(3)	No	Yes
(4)	No	No

Row (4) can be taken as a schema for radical skepticism. Is any epistemology today like this? Probably not. It is worth noting, however, that there is in some quarters a renewal of enthusiasm for a Nietzschean attack on "Appollonian" forms of knowing. In the case of Nietzsche himself, Habermas argues, the great German "philosopher with a hammer" presumed that a nineteenth-century positivist philosophy of science stated adequately the conditions of truth. Noting thereafter that such a conception could not offer a rational guide for living, Nietzsche went on to despair not only of truth in science but of truth *tout court* (cf. *KI,* pp. 290–300). Something of this tendency seems present, to cite a current example, in the later work of the French philosopher of history, Michel Foucault, who now refers to his own books as "fictions" and as "lancets, or Molotov cocktails, or minefields" which he would like "to self-destruct after use, like fireworks" (cf. Megill 1975, esp. pp. 492–503).

Row (3) might be taken as a schema for Romanticism. Shelley could serve as poetic analogue to Schleiermacher's philosophy:

> Thou hast a voice, great Mountain, to repeal
> Large codes of fraud and woe; not understood
> By all, but which the wise, and great, and good
> Interpret, or make felt, or deeply feel.
> [*Mont Blanc*] □

Some religious philosophies adopt this pattern: "What availeth us the knowledge of such things as shall neither help us at the Day of Judgment if we know them, nor hurt us if we know them not?" writes the author of the *Imitation of Christ*.

The nineteenth-century Danish philosopher Kierkegaard is perhaps such a Romantic. There is, however, something other than sheer passionate refusal of truth in his work. In his diary he writes:

> I am accused of causing young people to acquiesce in subjectivity. Maybe, for a moment. But how would it be possible to eliminate all the phantoms of objectivity that act as an audience, etc., except by stressing the category of the separate individual. Under the pretext of objectivity the aim has been to sacrifice individualities entirely. That is the crux of the matter. [Kierkegaard 1960, pp. 101–102]

Kierkegaard reminds us that the issue in Row (3) is not well diagrammed in the flat opposition of 'yes' and 'no.' The relation between Columns *A* and *B* is a more subtle and challenging one. Kierkegaard is trying to come to grips with what is a key element in any epistemology: the relationship of the universal to the particular, of the common to the individual, of theory to practice. Row (3) really expresses a drift and hierarchy between Columns *A* and *B*. More accurately, it should read like this:

(3)   No  Yes

Row (2) might be taken as a schema for monomethodologism. If we recall the "cup of coffee" analogy mentioned in the introduction, we remember that

such mental activities as cluster around the understanding pole are thought to be stimuli or perhaps first
formulations of a notion, which then is taken over by
the activities of explanation proper. The row, then,
could be more accurately diagrammed like this:

(2)   Yes ◄────────── No

Row (1) may be taken as a schema for contemporary
philosophical hermeneutics. In the minds of the authors reviewed here there is a constructive relationship
between the two sides. This might be another way of
thinking of the "hermeneutic circle" at a general level
and not only at the level of some particular communication. Obviously the preferred term for labeling such
a notion is 'dialectics.' The row could be diagrammed
like this:

(1)   Yes ◄────────► Yes

The dialectical double arrow is meant to indicate
three important aspects of contemporary hermeneutics.
   One is that there is no such thing as presuppositionless knowing. Hermeneutics holds, on the one hand,
that purposive and intentional interests are inherently
involved in the naturalistic studies of the physical sciences and, on the other, that the predictable behavior,
or lack of it, of natural systems is inherently involved
in the way we conceive our purposes and choose
means to bring them to fruition. A somewhat abstract
way of putting this might be to say that, though each

side of the double arrow elects its own proper object and strategy of investigation, the logic of its research conceptually entails certain structural mental systems functioning on the other side of the arrow.

A second point is that, just as there is no uniform stance from which to begin thinking, so there is no uniform term in which to end it. Hermeneutics is willing to rethink the dialectical logic of Hegel but not to accept his conclusion of an absolute mind. This anti-idealist stance of contemporary hermeneutics means that it accepts the irreducible contingency both of the thinker's own strategies and of reality itself. A kind of truth, nevertheless, can emerge—a truth or certainty, to adapt a phrase of von Wright's, based partly on confidence (that we can make the world different from what it is) and partly on ignorance (of the extent to which causal ties operate in the world)—based, one is tempted to interpolate, partly on being and partly on nothingness.

The third point indicated by the device of the double arrow is hermeneutics' recognition that intentionality is present and operative and effective on both sides of the table—and in a dialectical way. This effectiveness might be resident in the social condition of the researcher (cf. Habermas and Winch) or in the very logic of his research activity (cf. von Wright), or in the choice and manner of the questions he addresses to experience (cf. Gadamer). The question is, whether we are or are not to have a way to reflect on the functioning of intentionality in a fashion which recognizes its distinctive role. If we are not, then of course there *is* no Row (1), and we are back to a choice among positivism, Romanticism, or skepticism.

Gadamer, Habermas,
Winch, von Wright

Let us turn now to some general remarks about the
individual hermeneuticists cited in this book. The
French philosopher Paul Ricoeur has observed the developments we have reported with more than passing
interest, and he can help us in our task. Ricoeur himself, in fact, might easily have been included in our
short list of hermeneutical thinkers. True, in his earlier
work he thought of hermeneutics in a traditional way
as a study of methods for interpreting difficult texts,
but he now agrees with the extension of hermeneutics
to a general epistemological sphere (cf. Ricoeur 1978,
pp. 88–96). In a general way, we will be guided by
Ricoeur's critique of the authors we have used while
adding some comments of our own.

In an article entitled "History and Hermeneutics,"
Ricoeur describes Gadamer's and Habermas's philosophies as the "ascending" and "descending" pathways
of hermeneutical reflection respectively (cf. Ricoeur
1973*a*). The metaphor already suggests Ricoeur's own
perception that the two directions should really be the
correlative ends of a single path. He contends, however, that neither Gadamer nor Habermas has found
the way in which this complementarity might be
worked out.

In the case of Gadamer, he agrees with the Heideggerian project of investigating the ontological conditions of the disclosure of truth. He maintains, however, that the particular theses chosen in their work
make "any return from ontology to the epistemological question about the status of the human sciences

impossible" (Ricoeur 1978, p. 125). Here Ricoeur echoes the critique which Gadamer himself makes of Kant. He also echoes to some degree the complaint of those—like E. D. Hirsch, for example—who contend that Gadamer's work gives no standard for distinguishing between legitimate and illegitimate interpretations. It is not that Ricoeur is adopting without further ado the view that the right standard is the one Hirsch adopts—the intention of the author—but that Gadamer's approach offers no foothold from which to work positively toward a more adequate or appropriate methodology of the human sciences. He has so *much* ignored the methodological status of the human sciences as to leave them no role in the discovery of truth. Ricoeur himself is traditionalist enough to maintain that the highest task of hermeneutics is still to offer the possibility of "a true arbitration among the absolutist claims of each of the interpretations" (Ricoeur 1974, p. 15). If one doesn't succeed in finding a way to do this, then one will not succeed in escaping subjectivism and one will not, in fact, check the advance of positivism into the area of the human sciences (cf. Ricoeur 1978, pp. 153–165). In short, we have the right and we have the need, argues Ricoeur, that Gadamer show us the way toward some sort of positive continuity between the ontological and the methodological conditions of truth.

Habermas's approach, by contrast (the "descending pathway") does actively involve the positive sciences and does lead toward an epistemology of methods (cf. Ricoeur 1976, p. 689). In several ways, Ricoeur appears to be sympathetic to Habermas's approach. For example, he agrees with the Freudian point that, as

Ricoeur phrases it, "instinct is anterior to awareness and volition" and that "the *I am* is more fundamental than the *I speak*" (cf. Ricoeur 1974, p. 265). In that sense, he agrees that interests are anterior to knowledge. Furthermore, he agrees with Habermas's more recent enthusiasm for linguistics as the privileged area in which to search out an epistemology of method. Ricoeur's own goal, in fact, is to work out a "transcendental semiology" (cf. Ricoeur 1974, p. 261). Finally, he seems to agree with the neo-Marxian point that symbolic functioning is the very birth—and therefore shaper—of man and society (cf. Ricoeur 1974, pp. 258–259). What then is missing in Habermas's thesis?

What is missing so far is a solid standpoint from which to justify critique. Habermas's ideal of keeping *theoria* and *praxis* together is an honorable one, but it presents him with a dilemma he has not succeeded in resolving. Either *praxis* is its own justification—which amounts to epistemological terrorism—or it finds a foundation in a *theoria* separate from itself—which reinstates the sort of idealism Habermas wants to avoid.

Perhaps Ricoeur's point could be put this way: Habermas has willy-nilly slipped into Dilthey's error (an error of omission rather than of commission, one could say) of identifying the problem of understanding with the problem of understanding *another* (cf. Ricoeur 1977, p. 132): that is, another's perhaps domineering or exploitative intention, subjectivity, mind— whether that other be an individual or an institution. He thinks, in too exclusive a sense, that the meaning of a transmission must be the meaning that other subjects have put there. As long as he thinks this, he will never succeed in escaping subjective—that is, uncritical—

assessments of truth. But, Ricoeur argues, if certain recent studies in linguistics are correct, it makes sense to say that just as there is in the individual a generic communicative competence which is anterior to and independent of a particular utterance (and Habermas agrees with that), so in a particular utterance there is at once a "participation" in the intentions of the speaker or hearer and—because the text is now independently "out there"—a kind of "distanciation" and independence from the particular references which the speaker or hearer actually had in mind. This last Ricoeur calls *"la chose du texte"*—a settling in of meaning of an ontological kind that no longer belongs either to the intentionality of its "sender" or of its "receiver" but to the being of the utterance itself (cf. Ricoeur 1978, p. 160). Semiology would be the study of such levels of meaning, and it is in this direction that Ricoeur thinks epistemology should be moving. In doing so, he believes, the Heideggerian project will be recovered. One will retain, with Gadamer, "a kind of obedience to the text" (Ricoeur 1978, p. 93); one will both uncover the ontological structures of meaning and perhaps succeed in giving an interpretation of a "sort of being-in-the-world unfolded in front of the text" (Ricoeur 1978, p. 40).

Ricoeur's own hypothesis, then, is that *"la chose du texte"* is at the same time a mode of reality (and so satisfies the "ascending pathway" toward ontology) and one whose possibilities we can best describe if we pay attention to the objective social sciences, in particular linguistics (and so satisfies the critical need for a "descending pathway"). While learning from the researches of such social sciences, however, Ricoeur insists that one should not adopt their methods. These may be appropriate for limited ends but, by their bracketing the subject, they forbid themselves the possibility of an adequate effort to describe what it means for the subject to attempt to overcome "the closures of the universe of signs, in the intention of saying something about something to someone" (Ricoeur 1968, p. 119). Ricoeur's own philosophical recommendation is that we continue searching for some dialectical method in which "explanation and understanding would not constitute the extremes of an exclusionary relationship but would be the related moments of a complex process that one could call interpretation" (Ricoeur 1977, p. 127). If we can find this, we will have a form of knowing in which the subject will possess truth both in the manner of a participation and in the manner of a truth critically reached.

Let us turn to Winch. His analysis has something in common with that of the other three thinkers. With Gadamer he shares a sense of the linguisticality of man and is skeptical of being able to grant to methodology a secure control. He is also vulnerable to some of the charges of relativism made as well against Gadamer. In answering such charges, Winch veers further, it seems to me, in the direction of Gadamer's Aristotelian notion of a "resistance" or *logos* that may limit the options of development, at least practically.

This idea of a limiting concept points as well in the direction of a Chomskyan "deep structure" or "universal grammar" and is, therefore, allied to some degree with the thought of the later Habermas. Winch also shares Habermas's sense of the epistemological status of the whole process of socialization, but he is

more skeptical than Habermas of finding some constant human ideal by which to measure progress.
Where Habermas sees society as an exercise in a philosophy of history, Winch sees it as a kind of consuming
"logicality," so to call it, which, because we are in it,
we have no means of subjecting to effective critique.

It is noticeable that thinkers as different as Habermas, Ricoeur, and even Winch to a degree, all awaken
thoughts of a Chomskyan kind of deep structure
which may serve as an effective a priori in their epistemology and protect them from utter relativism. But it
is worth keeping in mind that Chomsky's own concept of an innate competence is a hypothesis developed
to explain certain empirical data: the almost infinitely
generative features of language performance. It is not
clear that the three thinkers mentioned have the sorts
of empirical data they would need in order to hypothe-
size their own forms of deep structure or ideal speech
situations. The reason is, of course, that the data they
need would be in the area of truth, justice, or
freedom—in short, in the area of ideals and purposes
and of the way things *should be,* not necessarily of the
way they *are.* In effect, then, these thinkers operate
with an assumption—a *Vor-Wissen,* as both von
Wright and Gadamer call it—which is a part of one's
tradition or *praxis* in life and simply cannot be brought
to adequate critique.

This observation returns us to the Wittgensteinian
point made by von Wright in the beginning of his
analysis; namely, that we start philosophizing with a
selection of guiding principles that are beyond
justification and in a sense beyond truth. What reality
may lie behind such principles exists in an area of

"noumenal ideas." The modesty of von Wright's approach gives it a certain strength: one need not make a commitment to transcendentalism in order to begin thinking. At the same time, it does make a positive connection with hermeneutical trends in continental philosophy.

This is because von Wright recognizes the need to develop a logic of action. This has two corollaries from the point of view of a history of ideas. One is that his work has promoted an effort to establish a logic for process—at least for one form of human process. In this it renews a part of Hegel's project. Another is that it has restored to an essential place in this logic the role of the subject. In this it renews a part of the project of Dilthey. This is a somewhat surprising and gratifying development, and Ricoeur has noted its promise (Ricoeur 1977). It confirms the thesis that the German philosopher Karl-Otto Apel argued in the study referred to earlier, to the effect that Anglo-Saxon preoccupations with problems of meaning were bound to lead to the sorts of questions taken up by Continental philosophy (Apel 1967).

At the same time there is a strength—again, relative simply to the current mix of ideas—in von Wright's analysis, because of the particular strategy he adopts. After all, logical empiricism can object against Continental philosophies what they so often object against each other—that they lapse into idealism. But empiricists, of whatever kind, cannot escape von Wright. His reflections begin from a standpoint internal to methodological attempts to offer explanations. Giving logic the "constant control" over his research, he shows that to explain in a way backed up by evidence conceptually involves an understanding that we can make the world different from what it is. Intentionality in practice, then—even intentionalities to explain—is the awareness of an interplay of causes and purposes. Causes bring about situations that, given a set of purposes, lead agents to act in ways that cause new situations and so trigger other sets of purposes, and so on. There is a constant dialectic between such causes and purposes. In his manner of working this relationship through, von Wright, it seems to me, may have succeeded in introducing Hegel into Wittgenstein's world. If so, he will have succeeded in allying the two most far-reaching influences of modern philosophy.

One may have the impression, from all that has been said, that philosophical hermeneutics turns to positivism a face set in the rigid mien of *"une fin à non-recevoir."* I hope I have indicated enough to show that this is not dogmatically the case. It would, in fact, be truer to say that positivism, by its own development, by its way of isolating, framing, and trying to solve problems of language, has been a decisive and progressive influence in the growth of hermeneutics. This was so in Dilthey's time. It is still true today. To the degree that positivism has provoked hermeneutics into rethinking itself it is now hermeneutics' turn to provoke positivism to the investigation of its own presuppositions. A dialogue is possible. A remark from one of Gilbert Ryle's papers seems appropriate:

> If there is more than one method of philosophy, or more than one strand in the method of philosophizing, the reveal-

ing of a new method or a new strand in the method is one of the biggest sorts of discovery that a philosopher can make.

However, that a proposed or exhibited method is a proper method or the proper method, or part of the proper method of philosophizing, is not a truth of private revelation, or a matter of personal taste. It is a philosophical proposition, and one on a question of 'principle.' So a school which claimed to be, and alone to be, on the right track in virtue of its monopoly of the true Method would only be a special case of what we considered before, the pretended monopoly of philosophical principles. The rival sects would again be separated only by rival pretensions, unless they join in exploring the case for and the case against those pretensions. And then they are not rivals. [Ryle 1937, p. 332]

Selected Bibliography

Abel, Reuben. 1976. *Man is the Measure: A Cordial Invitation to the Central Problems of Philosophy*. New York: The Free Press.

Abel, Th. 1953. "The Operation Called *Verstehen*," in Feigl, 1953. Pp. 677–687.

Anscombe, G. E. M. 1957. *Intention*. Ithaca: Cornell University Press.

Apel, Karl-Otto. 1967. *Analytic Philosophy of Language and the Geisteswissenschaften*. New York: Humanities Press.

Apel, Karl-Otto, Manninen, J., and Tuomela, R., eds. 1978. *Neue Versuche über Erklären und Verstehen*. Frankfurt am Main: Suhrkamp Verlag.

Bauman, Zygmunt. 1978. *Hermeneutics and Social Science*. New York: Columbia University Press.

"Bibliographical Guide to Hermeneutics and Critical Theory," 1975, *Cultural Hermeneutics*, 2: 379–390.

Borger, R., and Cioffi, F. 1970. *Explanation and the Behavioural Sciences*. Cambridge: Cambridge University Press.

Brodbeck, May, ed. 1968. *Readings in the Philosophy of the Social Sciences*. New York: Macmillan.

Bubner, Rüdiger, et al., eds. 1970. *Hermeneutik und Dialektik*. 2 vols. Tübingen: J. C. B. Mohr.

———. 1975. "Theory and Practice in the Light of the Hermeneutic–Criticist Controversy," *Cultural Hermeneutics*, 2: 337–377.

———. 1976. "Is Transcendental Hermeneutics Possible?" in Manninen, 1976. Pp. 59–77.

Chomsky, Noam. 1968. *Language and Mind*. New York: Harcourt, Brace, Jovanovich.

———. 1975. *Reflections on Language*. New York: Pantheon.

Comte, Auguste. 1896. *The Positive Philosophy of Auguste Comte*. Freely translated and condensed by Harriet Martineau. With an Introduction by Frederic Harrison. 3 vols. London: George Bell and Sons.

Cornelius, David K., and Vincent, Edwin St., eds. 1964. *Cultures in Conflict: Perspectives on the Snow–Leavis Controversy*. Chicago: Scott, Foresman, and Co.

Dallmayr, W. 1972. "Critical Theory Criticized: Habermas' *Knowledge and Human Interests* and Its Aftermath," *Philosophy of the Social Sciences,* 2: 211–229.

Dallmayr, W., and McCarthy, T., eds. 1977. *Understanding and Social Inquiry.* Notre Dame: Notre Dame University Press.

Danto, Arthur C. 1965. *Analytical Philosophy of History.* Cambridge: Cambridge University Press.

————. 1973. *Analytical Philosophy of Action.* Cambridge: Cambridge University Press.

Davidson, Donald. 1963. "Actions, Reasons, and Causes," *Journal of Philosophy,* 60: 685–700.

Dilthey, Wilhelm. 1914–. *Gesammelte Schriften.* 18 vols. Stuttgart: B. G. Teubner (vols. 1–12); Göttingen: Vandenhoek and Ruprecht (vols. 13–18).

————. 1961. *Meaning in History: W. Dilthey's Thoughts on History and Society.* Edited and introduced by H. P. Rickman. London: George Allen & Unwin, Ltd.

————. 1972. "The Rise of Hermeneutics," translated by Frederic Jameson. *New Literary History: A Journal of Theory and Interpretation,* 3: 229–244.

————. 1976. *W. Dilthey: Selected Writings.* Edited, translated, and introduced by H. P. Rickman. London: Cambridge University Press.

Dray, William. 1957. *Laws and Explanation in History.* New York and London: Oxford University Press.

Ermarth, Michael. 1975. *Wilhelm Dilthey: The Critique of Historical Reason.* Chicago and London: University of Chicago Press.

Fay, Brian. 1975. *Social Theory and Political Practice.* London: George Allen & Unwin, Ltd.

Feigl, Herbert. 1949. "Logical Empiricism." In Herbert Feigl and Wilfrid Sellars, eds. *Readings in Philosophical Analysis.* New York: Appleton-Century-Crofts, Inc. Pp. 3–26.

Feigl, Herbert, and Brodbeck, May, eds. 1953. *The Philosophy of Science.* New York: Appleton-Century-Crofts, Inc.

Fløistad, Guttorm. 1973. "Understanding Hermeneutics," *Inquiry,* 16: 445–465.

Føllesdal, Dagfinn. 1972. "An Introduction to Phenomenology for Analytic Philosophers." In R. E. Olson and A. M. Paul, eds.

Contemporary Philosophy in Scandinavia. Baltimore: Johns Hopkins Press.

Gadamer, Hans-Georg. 1967–1972. *Kleine Schriften.* 3 vols. Tübingen: J. C. B. Mohr.

—————. 1971. "Rhétorique, herméneutique, et critique de l'idéologie," *Archives de Philosophie,* 34: 207–230.

—————. 1972. "Hermeneutik als praktische Philosophie." In M. Riedel, ed. *Zur Rehabilitierung der praktischen Philosophie.* Freiburg: Rombach, 1: 325–344.

—————. 1975*a. Wahrheit und Methode: Grundzüge einer philosophischen Hermeneutik.* 3d ed. Tübingen: J. C. B. Mohr. English translation *Truth and Method.* New York: Seabury Press.

—————. 1975*b.* "Hermeneutics and Social Science," *Cultural Hermeneutics,* 2: 307–336.

—————. 1976. *Philosophical Hermeneutics.* Translated and edited by David E. Linge. Berkeley, Los Angeles, London: University of California Press.

—————. 1980. *Dialogue and Dialectic: Eight Hermeneutical Studies on Plato.* Translated with an Introduction by P. Christopher Smith. New Haven and London: Yale University Press.

Goldmann, L. 1969. *The Human Sciences and Philosophy.* London: Cape.

Habermas, Jürgen. 1970*a.* "On Systematically Distorted Communication," *Inquiry,* 13: 205–218.

—————. 1970*b.* "Towards a Theory of Communicative Competence," *Inquiry,* 13: 360–375.

—————. 1971. *Knowledge and Human Interests.* Translated by Jeremy J. Shapiro. Boston: Beacon Press.

—————. 1973. *Theory and Practice.* Translated by John Viertel. Boston: Beacon Press.

—————. 1974. "Habermas Talking: An Interview" (with Boris Frankel), *Theory and Society,* 1: 37–58.

—————. 1975. "A Postscript to *Knowledge and Human Interests,*" *Philosophy of the Social Sciences,* 3: 157–189.

—————. 1976. "The Analytical Theory of Science and Dialectics." In T. Adorno et al., eds. *The Positivist Dispute in German Sociology.* New York: Harper. Pp. 131–162.

—————. 1977. "A Review of Gadamer's *Truth and Method.*" In Dallmayr and McCarthy, 1977. Pp. 335–363.

———. 1979. *Communication and the Evolution of Society.* Translated with an Introduction by Thomas McCarthy. Boston: Beacon Press.

Hegel, G. W. F. 1931. *The Phenomenology of Mind.* Translated, with an Introduction and Notes by J. B. Baillie. 2d ed. London and New York: Macmillan.

Heidegger, Martin. 1962. *Being and Time.* Translated by John Macquarrie and Edward Robinson. London: SCM Press.

Heijenoort, Jean van. 1967. "Logic as Calculus and Logic as Language," *Synthese,* 17: 324–330.

Hempel, Carl. 1949. "The Function of General Laws in History." In Feigl, 1949. Pp. 459–471.

Hempel, Carl, and Oppenheim, Paul. 1953. "The Logic of Explanation." In Feigl, 1953. Pp. 319–352.

Hilpinen, Risto, ed. 1971. *Deontic Logic: Introductory and Systematic Readings.* Dordrecht: D. Reidel.

Hintikka, Jaakko. 1973. *Logic, Language Games, and Information.* Oxford: Clarendon Press.

———. 1975. *The Intentions of Intentionality and Other New Models for Modalities.* Dordrecht: D. Reidel.

———, ed. 1976. *Essays on Wittgenstein in Honor of G. H. von Wright.* Acta Philosophica Fennica, vol. 28, nos. 1–3.

Hirsch, Eric D., Jr. 1967. *Validity in Interpretation.* New Haven and London: Yale University Press.

———. 1978. *The Aims of Interpretation.* Chicago: University of Chicago Press.

Hoy, David Couzens. 1978. *The Critical Circle: Literature, History, and Philosophical Hermeneutics.* Berkeley, Los Angeles, London: University of California Press.

Ihde, Donald. 1971. *Hermeneutic Phenomenology: The Philosophy of Paul Ricoeur.* Evanston: Northwestern University Press.

Kant, Immanuel. 1968. *Immanuel Kant's Critique of Pure Reason.* Translated by Norman Kemp Smith. New York: St. Martin's Press.

Kenny, A. J. 1965. *Action, Emotion, and Will.* London: Routledge and Kegan Paul.

———. 1966. "Practical Inference," *Analysis,* 26: 65–75.

Kierkegaard, Søren. 1960. *The Diary of Søren Kierkegaard.* Translated by Gerda M. Anderson. Edited by Peter P. Rohde. New York: Philosophical Library.

Kraft, Viktor. 1953. *The Vienna Circle and the Origin of Neo-Positivism: A Chapter in the History of Recent Philosophy.* Translated by Arthur Pap. New York: Philosophical Library.

Kuhn, Th. 1962. *The Structure of Scientific Revolutions.* Chicago: University of Chicago Press.

Linge, David E. 1973. "Dilthey and Gadamer: Two Theories of Historical Understanding," *Journal of American Academy of Religion,* 41: 536–553.

Louch, A. R. 1966. *Explanation and Human Action.* Berkeley and Los Angeles: University of California Press.

McCarthy, Thomas. 1973. "On Misunderstanding Understanding," *Theory and Decisions,* 3: 351–370.

———. 1978. *The Critical Theory of Jürgen Habermas.* Cambridge and London: MIT Press.

Makkreel, Rudolf A. 1975. *Dilthey, Philosopher of the Human Studies.* Princeton: Princeton University Press.

Manninen, Juha. 1976. With Raimo Tuomela, eds. *Essays on Explanation and Understanding: Studies in the Foundations of Humanities and Social Sciences.* Dordrecht and Boston: D. Reidel.

Megill, Allan. 1979. "Foucault, Structuralism, and the Ends of History," *Journal of Modern History,* 51: 451–503.

Mill, John Stuart. 1884. *A System of Logic, Ratiocinative and Deductive: Being a Connected View of the Principles of Evidence and the Methods of Scientific Investigation.* 8th ed., New York: Harper and Bros.

Misgeld, Dieter. 1976. "Critical Theory and Hermeneutics: The Debate between Habermas and Gadamer." In O'Neill, 1976. Pp. 164–183.

Nielsen, Kai. 1973. "Social Science and Hard Data," *Cultural Hermeneutics,* 1: 115–143.

O'Neill, John, ed. 1976. *On Critical Theory.* New York: Seabury Press.

Palmer, Richard E. 1969. *Hermeneutics: Interpretation Theory in Schleiermacher, Dilthey, Heidegger, and Gadamer.* Evanston: Northwestern University Press.

———. 1973. "Phenomenology as Foundation for a Post-Modern

Philosophy of Literary Interpretation," *Cultural Hermeneutics*, 1: 207–223.

Parsons, Talcott. 1951. *Towards a General Theory of Action*. Cambridge: Harvard University Press.

Pettit, Philip. 1975. *The Concept of Structuralism: A Critical Analysis*. Berkeley, Los Angeles, London: University of California Press.

Radnitzky, Gerard. 1968. *Contemporary Schools of Metascience: Anglo-Saxon Schools of Metascience, Continental Schools of Metascience*. 2 vols. in 1, Göteborg: Akademiförlaget.

Ricoeur, Paul. 1968. "Structure, Word, Event," *Philosophy Today*, 12: 114–129.

———. 1970. "Qu'est-ce qu'un texte?" In Bubner, 1970. Pp. 181–200.

———. 1973a. "Ethics and Culture: Habermas and Gadamer in Dialogue," *Philosophy Today*, 17: 153–165.

———. 1973b. "Herméneutique et critique des idéologies." In Enrico Castelli, ed. *Démythisation et idéologie*. Paris: Aubier. Pp. 25–61.

———. 1974. *The Conflict of Interpretations: Essays in Hermeneutics*. Edited by Don Ihde. Evanston: Northwestern University Press.

———. 1976. "History and Hermeneutics," *Journal of Philosophy*, 73: 683–695.

———. 1977. "Expliquer et compredre. Sur quelques connexions remarquables entre la théorie du texte, la théorie de l'action et la théorie de l'histoire," *Revue philosophique de Louvain*, 75: 126–147.

———. 1978. *The Philosophy of Paul Ricoeur: An Anthology of His Work*. Edited by Charles E. Reagan and David Steward. Boston: Beacon Press.

Riedel, Manfred. 1978. *Verstehen oder Erklären: zur Theorie und Geschichte der hermeneutischen Wissenschaften*. Stuttgart: Klett-Cotta.

Riley, G. 1974. *Values, Objectivity, and the Social Sciences*. Reading, Mass.: Addison-Wesley.

Robinson, James M. 1964. With John B. Cobb, Jr., eds. *The New Hermeneutic*. New York: Harper and Row.

Ryle, Gilbert. 1937. With Margaret Macdonald and Isaiah Berlin.

"Symposium: Induction and Hypothesis," *Artistotelian Society: Supplementary Vol. XVI,* Pp. 36–62.

Ryle, Gilbert, et al. 1957. *The Revolution in Philosophy.* London: Macmillan.

Sensat, Julius, Jr. 1979. *Habermas and Marxism: An Appraisal.* Beverly Hills and London: Sage Publications.

Skjervheim, Hans. 1959. *Objectivism and the Study of Man.* Oslo: Universitetsforlaget.

Snow, C. P. 1969. *The Two Cultures: And a Second Look.* Cambridge: Cambridge University Press.

Tar, Zoltan. 1977. *The Frankfurt School: The Critical Theories of Max Horkheimer and Theodor W. Adorno.* New York: John Wiley and Sons.

Taylor, Charles. 1964. *The Explanation of Behavior.* New York: Humanities Press.

———. 1970. "Explaining Action," *Inquiry,* 13: 54–89.

———. 1971. "Interpretation and the Sciences of Man," *Review of Metaphysics,* 25: 3–51.

Tuomela, Raimo. 1977. *Human Action and Its Explanation: A Study on the Philosophical Foundations of Psychology.* Dordrecht and Boston: D. Reidel.

Waelhens, Alphonse de. 1962. "Sur une herméneutique de l'herméneutique," *Revue philosophique de Louvain,* 60: 573–591

Wax, M.␣L. 1967. "On Misunderstanding *Verstehen:* A Reply to Abel," *Sociology and Social Research,* 51: 323–333.

Wiggershaus, R., ed. 1975. *Sprachanalyse und Soziologie.* Frankfurt an Main: Suhrkamp.

Winch, Peter. 1958. *The Idea of Social Science and Its Relation to Philosophy.* London: Routledge and Kegan Paul.

———. 1969. "Introduction: the Unity of Wittgenstein's Philosophy," in *Studies in the Philosophy of Wittgenstein.* New York: Humanities Press. Pp. 1–19.

———. 1972. *Ethics and Action.* London: Routledge and Kegan Paul.

Wittgenstein, Ludwig. 1967*a. Ludwig Wittgenstein und der Wiener Kreis: Shorthand Notes Recorded by F. Waismann.* B. F. McGuiness, ed. Oxford: Basil Blackwell.

———. 1967*b. Zettel.* G. E. M. Anscombe and G. H. von Wright,

eds. Translated by G. E. M. Anscombe. Oxford: Basil Blackwell.

———. 1968. *Philosophical Investigations*. Translated by G. E. M.
Anscombe. Oxford: Basil Blackwell.

———. 1969. *On Certainty*. G. E. M. Anscombe and G. H. von
Wright, eds. Translated by Denis Paul and G. E. M. Anscombe.
New York and Evanston: J. and J. Harper.

Wolff, Janet. 1975. *Hermeneutic Philosophy and the Sociology of Art:
An Approach to some of the Epistemological Problems of the Sociology
of Knowledge and the Sociology of Art and Literature*. London and
Boston: Routledge and Kegan Paul.

Wright, Georg Henrik von. 1963a. *The Logic of Preference: An
Essay*. Edinburgh: The University Press.

———. 1963b. *Norm and Action: A Logical Enquiry*. New York:
Humanities Press.

———. 1971. *Explanation and Understanding*. Ithaca: Cornell University Press.

———. 1972. "Wittgenstein on Certainty," in *Problems in the Theory of Knowledge*. The Hague: Martinus Nijhoff. Pp. 47–60.

———. 1974. *Causality and Determinism*. New York and London:
Columbia University Press.

———. 1976a. "Replies," in Manninen and Tuomela, eds. Pp.
371–413.

———. 1976b. "Determinism and the Study of Man." In Manninen and Tuomela, eds. Pp. 415–435.

Zaner, Richard M. 1974. "A Certain Rush of Wind: Misunderstanding Understanding in the Social Sciences," *Cultural Hermeneutics*, 1:383–402.

Index

Designer: Steve Renick
Compositor: Innovative Media Inc.
Printer: Thomson-Shore, Inc.
Binder: Thomson-Shore, Inc. / John H. Dekker & Sons
Text: VIP Bembo
Display: Phototypositor Bembo